COUNSELLING CHILDREN AND YOUNG PEOPLE IN PRIVATE PRACTICE

COUNSELLING CHILDREN AND YOUNG PEOPLE IN PRIVATE PRACTICE
A Practical Guide

Rebecca Kirkbride

KARNAC

First published in 2016 by
Karnac Books Ltd
118 Finchley Road
London NW3 5HT

British Library Cataloguing in Publication Data

A C.I.P. for this book is available from the British Library

ISBN-13: 978-1-78220-261-5

Typeset by V Publishing Solutions Pvt Ltd., Chennai, India

Printed in Great Britain

www.karnacbooks.com

To R. S and P. C. K

CONTENTS

CONTENTS

INTRODUCTION

This book has grown out of more than a decade of working therapeutically with children and young people, both in private practice and other settings, during which time I have been struck by a sense of just how different the work is for the private practitioner with this group. The therapist working with children as part of their private practice has many important factors to consider including managing the relationship with parents, confidentiality and risk, and working with other professionals, among many others. This book is intended to offer assistance to the therapist who is grappling with these considerations. It is hoped that it will offer guidance and support to practitioners, who are perhaps already competent as therapists in other settings or in therapeutic work with adults, but who also have some interest in and may already be struggling with extending their private practice to include younger clients, as well as to those practitioners with less clinical experience but with an interest in this area.

Working therapeutically in private practice with children and their families can be a rewarding experience, but it can also be one fraught with concerns for practitioners, particularly around areas such as child protection and risk. These concerns can sometimes be off-putting to the extent that many practitioners with experience and knowledge in the field prefer to work only in school, college, or statutory or voluntary agency services. This book is intended as a support for any counselling or therapy practitioner who is considering or has considered working with children and young people in their private practice. It does not profess to be a textbook on child or adolescent development, or a comprehensive book on the theories underpinning child and adolescent psychotherapy or the techniques involved in delivering it. In this book I will be examining and exploring the professional issues that I, and other colleagues, have encountered while working in this field, while attempting to bring some clarity to the process of setting up a private practice with children and young people, as well as looking ahead to areas of potential conflict and difficulty which may arise once such a practice has been established.

Origins of therapeutic work with children

Counselling and psychotherapy, although developed initially as ways of treating or helping those experiencing difficulties in adulthood, have long been used as methods to approach and help those struggling earlier on in their lives. In 1909, Freud published his famous case study of the analysis of "Little Hans" (Freud, 1909b), a five-year-old boy he had treated for a phobia of horses. Although Freud himself did not pursue the development of child psychoanalysis, his daughter Anna and the psychoanalyst Melanie Klein went on to later develop two separate schools of thought and practice regarding the psychoanalytic treatment of children (Glenn, 1992).

Freud's early theories of psychoanalysis were based on his view that the development of the adult's personality belongs firmly in his childhood (Freud, 1923). His was a theory of instinctual drives which, when able to proceed appropriately, will lead to the development of a healthy adult able to engage in life, love, and work with enjoyment and a sense of satisfaction, as well as being able to deal with life's frustrations and vicissitudes without experiencing a total collapse. Freud recognised that the issues which adults faced in these areas had mostly originated in their childhoods so he set about studying and treating these origins via psychoanalysis (Freud, 1916[1915]). In this way he brought the importance of the experiences of childhood and children into the foreground of contemporary thought where, to some extent, they have remained. Later, the formation of the object-relations school led to the development of theories based, not only on the original drive theories expounded by Freud, but on an emphasis on the importance of the infant-mother relationship on the development of the personality (Fairbairn, 1952). Many of the theorists and clinicians, such as Bion, Winnicott, and Bowlby, practising and writing in the early and mid twentieth century were increasingly concerned with the impact of the environment and early relationships on child development. In the meantime, Anna Freud and Melanie Klein were treating children psychoanalytically and writing on the subject for other clinicians and those wishing to train in the field of child analysis.

Since this time, much has been written on the subject, and a variety of methods of working therapeutically with children and young people have developed. What has been clear throughout this time is that children and adolescents require methods of working which differ from those employed in adult therapy. There are a number of reasons for this, at the heart of which is the tension between their continued dependence upon their parents, along with the need to successfully develop to a point where separation and individuation from the family is a possibility. This book represents an attempt to explore this tension as it presents in counselling children and adolescents in a private practice setting.

There are many reasons why the practice of child psychotherapy and counselling has continued to develop. In terms of children's education, it has been increasingly recognised that children learn more effectively in school when their emotional needs are met and they have obtained a general level of security in themselves and their environment, enabling them to feel safe enough to engage with their education (Geddes, 2006; Salzberger-Wittenberg, Henry, & Osborne, 1983). Children are increasingly viewed as being able to benefit, in this and other respects, from therapeutic interventions, and there is a growing body of research and literature to support this view (Fonagy et al., 2014). Society as a whole now seems increasingly prepared to recognise that if children who are struggling emotionally and psychologically are helped early on, they are likely to cope far better as adults and be less likely to become dependent upon medical and other services in later life. They may even be happier, as well as more productive members of society!

There has also been some expansion in the settings where therapy is offered to children and young people. As well as the NHS (National Health Service) in the UK offering therapeutic interventions via in—and outpatient services, and CAMHS (Child and Adolescent Mental Health

Service), there has been a massive expansion in counselling provided in school and college settings in the last twenty years. There are also more children's' charities promoting and offering therapy through voluntary and third sector organisations. However, with NHS CAMHS provision often heavily oversubscribed, and school and college services increasingly only offering brief therapeutic interventions, more and more parents are likely to seek out private counsellors and therapists for their children. Private practice is a unique setting for children's therapy, offering opportunities for a variety of interventions, brief or longer term therapy, without the strict criteria or agendas of statutory settings.

Chapter contents

This book is divided into four main parts covering the practical, ethical, and professional aspects of working therapeutically with children and young people in private practice. The fourth part is a stand-alone chapter which examines recent developments regarding the impact of digital technology and cyber culture on young people, therapy, as well as the therapists themselves.

Having worked in private practice, agency, and educational settings as a therapist, it is has become apparent to me that working in private practice with children and adolescents brings practitioners into contact with dilemmas largely absent from similar work with adults, and which also tends to not be present in educational or other organisational settings. Chief amongst these is the issue around the presence of the parent in the therapy with children. In private practice the parent or carer must be considered as an "other" in the therapeutic relationship, even if they are not a constant presence in the therapy room. How much involvement this "other" party has in the therapy will, of course, depend on a large number of factors. For example, a young child might need to have their parents physically present in some capacity for at least part of the early phase of the therapeutic work, whereas an older teenager is likely to be much more autonomous in their engagement with their counselling. This negotiation of the relationship between client, parental figures, and therapist can be complex and delicate and it can also need to change over time. Working in private practice can enable us to work much longer term than other settings might give scope for and this can mean that a young client can move through developmental stages while they are undergoing therapy. A client who begins therapy as a fourteen-year-old and stays until they are sixteen or older will more than likely require flexibility and adaptation in the frame and contract over that time, as will a younger child moving into puberty and preadolescence.

Therapy generally begins with a referral and an assessment of some kind and this is of particular importance in work with this age group. Chapter One looks at the process of assessing children and young people for therapeutic work in private practice. The chapter covers the importance of considering developmental stages when assessing children and young people as well as introducing the fundamental concept of "Gillick" competency, a vital component of all therapeutic work with young people.

In Chapter Two, issues around contracting are explored including the issue of fees and who has "ownership" of the therapy and the right to set the agenda when the client and the person funding the therapy are not the same person. This brings up developmental and ethical issues around when, and to what degree, children have autonomy and the right to decide on their own treatment along with capacity for making decisions regarding their own desired therapeutic outcomes. It may be very difficult for a parent who is used to having control of their child's life to a large degree to allow their child's counselling to remain mysterious and confidential, especially when they are heavily financially and emotionally invested.

This part of the book also includes chapters on the practicalities of setting up a practice which can accommodate children and young people, including administrative as well as material requirements, and on working with parents and other family members, an important area for consideration in working with this group. Also considered in this chapter are the impact that divorce and separation can have on the therapy and how practitioners might manage issues arising from this when working with the children of split and/or "blended" families.

Part II of the book covers ethical issues in private practice with children, beginning with a look at ethics, the law and confidentiality. Just as in organisational and educational settings, work with children and young people requires consideration of and preparation for safeguarding and other ethical issues. Whereas in educational or statutory settings there are often policies in place regarding child protection, in private practice the onus is on the therapist themselves to develop their own policies regarding working with issues around risk and safeguarding children. Chapter Five explores the law and ethical guidelines as they relate to work in this area and provides a framework to enable to the practitioner to develop their own policies regarding safeguarding, confidentiality, and data protection.

Chapter Six looks at issues of risk which may emerge in therapeutic work with children and young people and at how these can be worked with ethically, maintaining the client's right to confidentiality but also keeping their welfare firmly in mind.

The third part of the book, which relates to professional issues of work in this field, focuses on working with other professionals and includes chapters on how practitioners might manage onward referrals to other professionals and agencies when appropriate and on the fundamentals of training and supervision, vital in providing the practitioner in private practice with the support to work confidently and ethically in this field.

The final part and chapter covers recent developments in digital technology and how these affect the lives of young people growing up today constantly connected to one another and cyberspace via their mobile devices. The chapter explores the impact these developments may have on the lives of young people and on what they bring into their sessions materially. The chapter looks briefly at research and developments in online therapy with young people and considers how a practitioner might think about their own personal and professional life in cyberspace.

I have chosen to illustrate much of the text throughout with vignettes and case studies intended to elucidate the text and bring some relevant areas of clinical work to life. The characters and situations in the case material are fabricated for the purposes of this book and do not resemble any actual clinical work undertaken. Any resemblance is purely coincidental.

There is often a lack of clarity regarding the professional titles employed by those working therapeutically. Throughout this book I use the terms "counsellor", "therapist", and "practitioner" interchangeably to denote a therapy professional trained or training in delivering confidential therapy and therapeutic interventions to individuals or groups of young people. I also use the term "children" to denote all those under eighteen years of age but include "young people" to identify that there is a difference between pre and post-adolescent children. This book is intended to cover therapeutic work with children aged up to eighteen years and therefore not legally adults. However there is much that will be relevant to those working with over-eighteen year olds who are still financially and/or materially dependent upon their parents as well as emotionally. I have chosen to use the term "client" to indicate anyone receiving therapy, rather than use "client" and "patient" interchangeably.

Finally, although this book positions itself as a "practical guide" in some respects it is in no way intended to act as a manual for the work. Practitioners will hopefully come to this text with a variety of ideas of their own as to how they might manage a private practice that can include children and young people and will find support in the text for their own decisions in this respect.

PART I

PRIVATE PRACTICE WITH CHILDREN AND YOUNG PEOPLE

CHAPTER ONE

Referral and assessment

In all therapeutic work, the referral and assessment stages can play a vital part in determining the shape and success of the therapy to follow. In work with children and young people in private practice this can be a complex aspect of the work which demands close attention and skill from the practitioner. Amongst other things, therapists must think about establishing a therapeutic relationship which includes parents or carers, assess and then consider the impact on the therapy of the developmental stage a child or young person has reached, as well as come to a decision regarding a client's capacity to consent to a confidential therapeutic relationship.

Throughout this chapter case vignettes will be used in order to give practical examples of how a practitioner might approach referral and assessment in their private practice.

Initial referral

Case material: Heather and Conor—Part One

Heather is a counsellor of children and young people in private practice. She receives a voicemail from Yasmin who is seeking counselling for her eleven-year-old son, Conor. In her message, Yasmin says that she found Heather's details in an online therapy directory. Yasmin expresses concerns about Conor's adjustment after her recent separation from his father. He appears anxious about going to school and is no longer enjoying his out of school activities such as football club and karate. She asks Heather to please call her to arrange an initial appointment.

Where therapy with children and young people in private practice differs significantly from work with adults is in the necessity for practitioners to have a relationship not only with the client but also with a third party, generally a parent or carer. This unique element of the work is one which will be referred to frequently throughout the chapters of this book as it represents a fundamental consideration in this area. Managing the complexity of a relationship with both the client and their parents can raise anxiety for practitioners, which is why close attention will be paid to it within these pages. From the first contact with a parent seeking therapy for their child, no matter what the child's age, the therapist needs to begin to build a rapport and relationship with the parent, enabling them to feel comfortable about bringing their child for counselling. Parents and carers will be wanting to get a sense of the therapist's warmth and approachability just as do prospective clients in adult practice. Any conversations or contact early on in the process between therapist and referrer provide an opportunity for parents to be given a sense of the potential for understanding and the positive outcome to be gained from therapy for their child. The therapist must, however, remain mindful that the adult here is not the client and that in the future, if the counselling goes ahead, they will be building a confidential therapeutic relationship with the child which the parent(s) will to some extent be excluded from. If this complex dynamic is not understood at this stage it can become difficult further on to offer the client a clear sense that the therapist is there for their benefit and is not simply another "parent-like" adult following an agenda based on the parents' wishes, with no consideration of the client's needs. The demand on the practitioner here is to skilfully manage to create an alliance with the referring parent but also to create and maintain boundaries which will allow for the provision of a neutral therapeutic space when work with the client begins.

Whichever terms are used to describe the referral and assessment phase of the therapeutic relationship; initial consultation, assessment, preliminary interview or history taking, many of the elements of the process will be similar. In, "Why assess", Tantam (1995) outlines the goals of the "first psychotherapeutic interview". These include; "establishing rapport with the patient", "obtaining pertinent information", "giving information", "enabling the patient to feel understood and giving hope", "giving the patient a taste of the treatment" and "making practical arrangements for therapy". "Why assess" was written with individual psychotherapy with adults in mind but these goals are clearly relevant to work with children and young people and their parents or families. However when assessing for work with the latter we need to think about the process slightly differently and take some other important factors into account.

The way the referral and assessment stages are managed with parents will depend to a large extent upon the age and developmental stage or phase that their child has reached. Throughout this book we will be examining how developmental stages will influence the form that therapy takes and this is of particular importance at assessment. Clearly the developmental needs and dependencies of a five-year-old are considerably more parent-centred than those of an eleven or seventeen-year-old. Parents are generally the driving force behind the therapy of younger children whereas post-puberty and during the individuation processes of adolescence, children may have a far greater sense of their own autonomy regarding their issues and some sense of the need for assistance in working with these. As Anna Freud (1965) writes;

> Some of the most lively controversies concerning the specificity of child analysis are related to the question whether and how far parents should be included in the therapeutic process. Although this is overtly a technical point, the issue at stake is a theoretical one, namely, the decision whether and from which point onward a child should cease to be considered as a product of and dependent on his family and should be given the status of a separate entity, a psychic structure in its own right. (A. Freud, 1965, p. 43)

Anna Freud goes on later in the same chapter to suggest that practitioners take note of not just a patient's chronological age but also of what use he makes of his parents in order to assess his state of "dependency or independence". She suggests; "… it is essential for the analyst to realize in which of the vital respects the child leans on the parents and how far he has outgrown them" (A. Freud, 1965, p. 46).

The following table illustrates the modes of relating to parents that Anna Freud suggests demonstrate a child or young person's state of dependency or independence.

Table 1.1. A. Freud—Developmental stages of dependency.

Uses that a child makes consecutively of his/her parents (A. Freud, 1965)	*How this might present at referral/ assessment*
For narcissistic unity with a motherly figure, at the age when no distinction is made between self and environment.	A child or young person who struggles in sustaining a separate sense of themselves in relation to the parent or others.
For leaning on their capacity to understand and manipulate external conditions so that body needs and drive derivatives can be satisfied.	A child or young person unsure of how they can exist without the help and support of a parent to keep them alive and functioning. No sense at this point of their own potential or resources in this respect. They may understand that they are not their parents at this stage but not that they could survive without them.
As figures in the external world to whom initially narcissistic libido can be attached and where it can be converted into object libido.	A child or young person who is developing an ongoing sense of themselves through their relationships and connections to others. Parents in this respect are connected with in order to be able to explore aspects of self and other relationships.
To act as limiting agents to drive satisfaction, thereby initiating the child's own mastery of the id.	A child or young person who is in need of externally provided boundaries to help them manage themselves and to develop a stable and functioning ego.
To provide the patterns for identification which are needed for building up an independent structure.	A child or young person who has a fairly well established sense of themselves internally but still requires external adult identifications to help their transition to independence from their parents.

It can be helpful when thinking about working with young clients to assess what stage they have reached in this respect and to consider whether a client is able to think about themselves and their experiences separately from how their parents think about them. It was twenty years after Anna Freud was writing about a child's right to be considered a separate entity that the legislative processes in the UK and elsewhere began to consider such concepts within the law regarding children's' rights, culminating in the establishment of "Gillick" competency.

Gillick competency

The "Gillick" case of 1985 was fundamental in the UK to helping practitioners in thinking about the parents' role in their child's therapy. This case gave rise to the term "Gillick Competency" and preceded the Children Act of 1989 which gave children further rights separate to their families' or the state's wishes for them. Victoria Gillick brought her case to the House of Lords when her local health authority failed to offer her assurance that none of her five daughters would be offered contraceptive advice or services prior to the age of sixteen without her permission. Her action followed the publication of a local authority information pamphlet suggesting that the prescribing of contraceptives to minors under sixteen be at the doctor's discretion rather than the parents'. When Gillick's case was rejected by the House of Lords the ruling meant that children had been acknowledged by law as independent of their parents. The Gillick case then gave rise to the Gillick test. In discussing the Gillick case, Daniels and Jenkins (2010) quote Lord Scarman as saying:

> ... the parental right to determine whether or not their minor child below the age of 16 will have medical treatment terminates if and when the child achieves a sufficient understanding and intelligence to enable him to understand fully what is proposed. (Gillick v. West Norfolk AHA, 1986, at 423) (Daniels & Jenkins, 2010, p. 19)

In private practice, where the referral is generally made by the parents or legal carers of a child or young person, there is no need to refer to

Gillick in terms of whether treatment can be offered as the referral itself implies parental consent. However, in terms of how an agenda for therapy is set, contracts made regarding confidentiality and record keeping, and how we involve parents in their child's therapy, Gillick and the general concept of capacity to give consent do have a relevance.

The Gillick ruling made it clear that anyone offering treatment to a child or young person must consider them able to make their own choices, without the knowledge or consent of their parents, regarding this treatment if they have reached a point of sufficient intellectual and emotional capability to do so. The practitioner is required to make this judgement and must feel confident in doing so.

The principles of Gillick have been adopted elsewhere around the world including in Australia, New Zealand, and Canada. In the US the law is more complex on the rights of minors to access confidential medical treatment and can vary from state to state. On the whole, most states have laws which recommend that children have access to confidential medical treatment from around the age of fourteen but that right is limited if the child is considered to be at significant risk of harm. There is a federal guideline within the "Patient Privacy Rule" which took effect in 2003 that states that parents should have access to "information about the health and well-being of their children" but this also states that "disclosure of health information about a minor child to a parent should be governed by state or other applicable laws" (Weisleder, 2004, p. 147). We will return to Gillick competency and the law around counselling children in Chapter Five.

Developmental models

There are some useful developmental models to consider when thinking about the assessment of children and young people for therapy. Jean Piaget, a Swiss psychologist, studied and wrote extensively throughout the 1920–1970s on the subject of children's' cognitive development. Piaget recognised that children's ability to think and make sense of their world went through different stages as they grew up. He saw children's thinking as going through four major developments as outlined below:

Table 1.2. Piaget's stages of cognitive development (1964).

Age	Developmental stage
Birth to two years	**Sensorimotor stage**—infants and babies experience the world through sense and action.
Two to six years	**Preoperational stage**—young children begin to represent and understand their experiences through words and images.
Seven to eleven years	**Concrete operational stage**—children are able to think logically about concrete happenings and make analogies between them.
Twelve years onwards	**Formal operational stage**—adolescents and young adults are able to consider hypothetical situations and process abstract, non-concrete, thoughts.

Considering clients at assessment in relation to these stages can help practitioners not only decide how to work therapeutically but also in understanding how able a particular child is to consent to and actively take part in decisions about their own therapy. Once a child has reached the formal operations stage they are more likely to be able to consider fully the implications of confidentiality in their counselling and be able to give informed consent in this respect.

Bowlby and attachment theory

Attachment theory, developed by John Bowlby (1973) during the 1940s and 1950s is also appropriate for use by practitioners when assessing children and young people for counselling. Bowlby was a psychiatrist and psychoanalyst who used ethological studies as the basis for understanding human development and relationships. He was particularly interested in the impact that any separation from their main caregiver had on young children's emotional and psychological development.

As Bowlby (1973) continued to explore the nature of children's attachments, his discoveries led him to conclude that in order to develop a secure attachment, children required a caregiver who was both psychologically and physically present as well as emotionally available. The effects of being raised by an emotionally or psychologically unavailable parent could be just as significant as temporary or permanent physical separation from the caregiver. Attachment theory suggests that the early experiences children have of their caregiver's ability to respond appropriately to their needs leads to the development of an "internal working model" (Ainsworth, Blehar, Waters & Wall, 1978), which then becomes a fundamental factor for the child, determining to a great extent how they will experience themselves and their relationships as they grow older. Early attachment experiences in this way are important in the building of a mental representation of the self, others, and the relationship between self and other. The child quickly begins to develop a sense of their own worthiness and acceptability to the other, as well as how reliably others and the world around them will meet their emotional and physical needs. Their behaviour is adaptive according to these discoveries, becoming the basis of strategies intended to help the child maintain proximity to their attachment figure and secure base. An example of this is when a child experiences their emotions as causing their parent to move away from them, and therefore begins to try to suppress or hide their true feelings from the parent in an attempt to prevent the feared abandonment.

While working with Bowlby on experiments aimed at observing and understanding children's attachment behaviour and patterns, Mary Ainsworth developed the "strange situation" test (Ainsworth, Blehar, Waters & Wall, 1978) for classifying children's attachment patterns at an early age. This test consisted of creating a situation in which mother and child are together, then a stranger enters the room, mother leaves and then returns after a short while. The reaction of the child to both the stranger, the separation from mother and her return were all monitored and then classified according to the attachment "pattern" they best fitted. Bowlby (1973) proposed that children were either securely or insecurely attached to their parent figure and that this attachment was an indicator of their capacity to develop and cope with separation and loss as they grew older and became adult. The behaviour of the child in this test indicated the adaptations they had made to their proximity seeking behaviour in order to maintain some sense of connection to their caregiver. Ainsworth took the results of the test and categorised them according to the behaviours exhibited as shown in table 1.3 below:

Table 1.3. Attachment patterns.

Attachment style	Caregiving experience	Presentation
Secure	Parent reliably responsive and attuned to infant/child's physical and emotional needs.	Child with a sense of trust that their needs will be recognised and responded to appropriately.
Insecure—Avoidant	Parent who is experienced as rejecting, interfering, and controlling. Child's distress seems to annoy or upset caregiver.	Child who denies or does not communicate their needs as they fear they will upset their caregiver by doing so. In older children and adolescents disavowed feelings and needs may be communicated in other, indirect ways such as self-harm and eating disorders.
Insecure—Ambivalent	Parent who is inconsistently available when needed by their child.	The child finds that they cannot guarantee the attention of the parent so they become preoccupied with obtaining it through anger, threats, and clinging behaviours. They may find friendships and relationships very difficult as they both want connection but are highly sensitive to whether they are connected to the other.
Insecure—Disorganised	A parent or caregiver who is the cause of distress to the infant or child. A parent who is significantly abusive or neglectful of their child's needs.	The child cannot find a way of having positive proximity to their caregiver and therefore they have no adult regulation of their feelings. They become distressed psychologically and display a mix of behaviours and may seem fearful and incoherent in times of stress.

Bowlby (1973) suggested that if a child had not managed to form a secure early attachment with their parent or caregiver they would be likely to struggle with separation and loss as they got older. They may struggle to attend school or to form friendships and other important connections. Issues relating to an insecure early attachment can present at any stage in a person's life including adulthood. It must also be noted that clients with issues forming secure attachments may also struggle in forming an attachment to their therapist. Children with an insecure attachment style may be very sensitive to signs that their therapist is not going to be able to provide a secure base for them and may find breaks in the therapy as well as beginnings and endings particularly difficult. It may be difficult for them to trust that the therapist will attend to the client in the room rather than being preoccupied by their own needs. If we can begin to have a sense at the assessment stage of where a client is in terms of their attachment patterns it can help us to be particularly sensitive to them in this respect.

These attachment categories can be used to assess not only the internal working model of a client but also the relationship between parent and child which can be helpful in exploring the origins of presenting issues and if the therapeutic work comes to include parents or other family members during its course.

Gathering information

Case material: Heather and Conor—Part Two

Heather returns Yasmin's phone call and arranges for them to meet in her consulting room to discuss Yasmin's concerns regarding Conor. When they meet Heather takes note of Yasmin's general appearance and demeanour, observing that she looks underweight and seems low to the point of depression. Yasmin is tearful during this initial meeting as she describes the recent separation from her husband who left after telling her that he no longer loves her. Yasmin tells Heather that Conor was a much longed for child who was born via IVF when she was thirty-seven. Her pregnancy went well but Conor's birth was difficult and she had to have an emergency caesarian delivery. After his birth, Yasmin experienced a period of post-partum depression when she felt disconnected from Conor and worried that she would not be able to care for him properly. At this point, her own mother was very supportive and spent some time looking after Conor while Yasmin rested and recovered from the birth. Conor's father was at work during this period and his daily commute meant that he was out of the house from 6am until 7 or 8pm, five days per week. At the weekends Conor spent a lot of time with his dad which they both enjoyed.

Yasmin says that Conor's early childhood was a relatively happy and settled time for the family. He was a healthy toddler who engaged with toilet-training well and who followed developmental lines in accordance with normal expectations.

Yasmin came out of her period of post-partum depression when Conor was about six months old and after that had no problem in developing a good relationship with her son. Conor also has a close relationship with his dad whom Yasmin describes as his idol. They enjoy playing and watching football together and Yasmin suspects that Conor's current difficulties may be connected to him missing his dad. Yasmin tells Heather that she feels angry with her ex-husband and devastated by his departure. She has noticed that Conor is becoming increasingly hostile towards her and seems to blame her for his dad's leaving. Conor no longer wants to play or watch football and is increasingly anxious in the mornings about going to school. Yasmin fears that Conor may start to refuse to go in to school. He currently spends alternate weekends with his dad who is busy during the week.

Heather decides with Yasmin that it would be a good idea if Yasmin brings Conor in and they meet for a while together and then Conor spends some time alone with Heather if he is happy to do so. Heather informs Yasmin about confidentiality regarding the sessions. Yasmin agrees that the sessions have to be confidential but also admits that she may have difficulty not knowing what Heather and Conor have spoken about. Heather says that she understands this and suggests a review of the counselling of some description after six sessions so that Yasmin has a sense of how the counselling is going. Heather also gives Yasmin an information sheet regarding what to expect once counselling begins.

When taking a referral for a child aged twelve or under who would not be considered to be "Gillick" competent it is important to meet with the parent(s) separately for an assessment session where a full history of the child and the family as a whole can be taken, along with the gathering of background information regarding the presenting issue. Neubauer (1992) describes this important aspect of the assessment as parent(s) and therapist forming an "information alliance" which "develops concomitant with the therapeutic alliance with the child" (Neubauer, 1992, p. 267). This "information alliance" can then be used to obtain information about the pregnancy and birth of the client as well as about other siblings within the family unit. Also important to gather is information regarding any experience the mother may have had of post-partum depression or other illness/debilitation. Practitioners need to approach this area with tact and sensitivity at the assessment. Many women feel enormous shame and confusion about a struggle to bond and/or ambivalent feelings towards their children in the post-partum period and this guilt or shame can linger under the surface many years after the depression has passed. However, research has shown that post-partum depression can have a major impact on emotional and neurological development in infants (Harvard University, 2009) and therefore can be an important factor in the aetiology of a symptom or behaviour. Gathering information about the wider family can be particularly useful at this point. Bereavements, moving house or other examples of upheaval and trauma can provide important indicators of how environmental factors may have affected the client and the family.

At referral, practitioners may find that parents are themselves experiencing anxiety and looking for support and containment of their own feelings and it can be difficult not to be affected by this. As Marks Mishne (1983) writes; "Clinicians must guard against becoming infected by parents' anxiety and giving premature opinions and recommendations" (Marks Mishne, 1983, p. 27). With parents who are themselves experiencing difficulties emotionally or psychologically which are affecting their children it can prove difficult for therapists to remain clear about who the client is. It can often appear to the counsellor that the worrying or disturbing behaviour the client is presenting with is a symptom of the distress or disturbance elsewhere in the family unit and therefore not just an issue for the individual client. The chapter on working with parents and families will look in more detail at how to work within the family system with the presenting issue. As is discussed in that chapter, some parents can be aware of the influence of family dynamics on the presenting issues and be able to talk about and work with this but others may be more defended and want to see their child's issues as totally separate from anything else which is happening within the family. This kind of denial can present difficulties for the practitioner as demonstrated in the following case example:

> Karen contacts a counsellor via email regarding counselling for her seven-year-old daughter, Maisie. Maisie has begun to develop phobias regarding eating certain foods, especially during family outings, although now she is also expressing concern about cleanliness and food preparation at home. Karen tells the counsellor that there is nothing she can think of which has changed at home recently or anything she can think might be raising Maisie's anxiety. She seems surprised that the counsellor would ask such a question. Karen has heard that CBT is very good for phobias and she hopes that this is something that can be offered by the counsellor. It is only after the counsellor has been seeing Maisie for several weeks that Karen mentions, again via email, that her husband has been having an affair and that they are in the process of separating. She is telling the counsellor this, she says, so she is aware that there might be "some awkwardness" between her and her husband at the next review. Maisie and her younger brother, she says, don't yet know that anything is going on.

During the initial assessment, when the therapist meets with the parent or carer of a pre-"Gillick" competent child and asks them for background information and family history they are asking them to "stand-in" for the client, who themselves is too young to have access to all the relevant information. The parents are being asked to give information regarding any major family events or historical incidents which may have had an impact or contributed to their child's development. They are asked this on the basis of the therapist wanting to provide their child with the most appropriate therapeutic intervention, not from a place of nosiness or judgement. It is therefore very important at this stage of the work to be clear with parents that the information they are giving is of relevance to their child's therapy but the information will not be used any other way. If material is uncovered in the course of the assessment that is distressing it may be useful to have the names of therapists available to suggest to the parent. This demonstrates an understanding by the therapist that there may be unresolved issues in the parents' own history which might benefit from some therapeutic support obtained outside of their child's therapy.

It is worth bearing in mind that, just as in assessment with adult clients, parents can be selective in what they share in the assessment and it is useful to remember that the story they tell is a version of the client's history and background rather than absolute fact.

Questionnaires

An alternative approach to this kind of history taking session with a parent or carer could be to use a questionnaire to gather the required background information. A general downside to this approach is that the information comes back in a somewhat one dimensional form. It also denies the practitioner the opportunity to pursue different avenues of information which may arise from a face-to-face assessment interview. A questionnaire may be a more appropriate tool when thinking about the assessment process for adolescent clients, which is covered further on in this chapter.

A taste of the treatment

Having met or spoken with the parent or carer of the prospective client and gathered the information necessary to decide whether this is an appropriate referral, the second part of the assessment process will be to meet with the child themselves.

In aiding this transition from the parental assessment to one with the child, parents can be helped to prepare their child. If, at the initial meeting or during an assessment phone conversation the practitioner has begun to form a good alliance with the parent then this preparation should be easier. If the parent is ambivalent or conflicted themselves about the therapy process it may be harder for them to help their child feel positive about the meeting. It is therefore of great importance that practitioners try to discuss and alleviate parents' anxieties regarding the therapy process as much as possible before the initial meeting with the child. Parents should also be encouraged to discuss the assessment with their child at an age appropriate level before the appointment takes place and in a way which is positive and supportive of the idea that the session is about helping the child with something they may have been finding difficult lately. Parents may ask for the practitioner's assistance in helping them think about how they might go about this preparation and it is important that the therapist be open to providing this help. In private practice, therapy is dependent to some extent upon the parent's support. With this in mind, any help offered by the therapist at this stage to help the parent feel secure in bringing their child to counselling is likely to be of great value to the work overall.

Apart from work with older adolescents, it will generally be necessary to have the parent present for the assessment for at least a part of the time, especially with younger children and sometimes with older ones too.

The arrival of client and parent for the assessment together is a good opportunity for the child or young person to see their parent interacting with the therapist as someone familiar to them and hopefully as someone in whom they have begun to develop some trust. This in turn should help to put the child at ease and allow them also to see the therapist as someone potentially safe and trustworthy. This meeting with child and parent can also provide a good opportunity to observe parent and child interactions and get a sense of the family dynamics. There are a variety of possible ways to approach this session although how the actual assessment is structured will depend a great deal on the individual practitioner's chosen method or clinical model. One suggestion might be to play a game together for part of the time. This provides an opportunity to observe parent–child dynamics in an atmosphere of relaxed play. This can also be very helpful in allowing the client to become familiar with the therapist and feel easier about the whole experience of coming for therapy. Having played for a while the child can then be asked if they would be ok talking with the therapist alone while mum or dad waits downstairs. This process is useful for allowing observation of how the child separates from their parent and vice versa. Once the parent has left, the therapist can begin to gain a sense from the child of what their understanding is regarding their coming for counselling. Do they understand that they are seeing a counsellor and what is their understanding of what that means? How do they understand themselves; are they a problem in need of fixing or are they just expecting to come and play with no real sense of the purpose of the meeting? Sometimes children have internalised a sense of the parents' problem with their behaviour but not have a sense of the difficulty themselves. They may recognise that their parent is unhappy with them in some way but they may not understand why. Alternatively, children and young people can feel invested and get significant relief from a symptom which is disturbing to the parent.

Marks Mishne (1986) identifies this as an issue often affecting work with adolescents. As she puts it;

> Often teenagers do not experience their symptoms as painful. When their self-injurious or maladaptive behaviors are ego-syntonic, rather than ego-dystonic, they do not experience anguish or anxiety. Rather the adults (namely, parents and teachers) suffer and commonly forcibly refer the adolescent for therapy. (Marks Mishne, 1986, p. 328)

Children and young people may potentially feel some hostility toward the therapist whom they perceive will be on the side of the parent who disapproves of their behaviour and wants to "take it away" from them. This can potentially interfere with the forming of the "therapeutic alliance" (Zetzel, 1956), and therefore with the success of the therapy altogether. A way of managing this could be to ask the child how they feel about the referral and about any concerns their parents have raised. Do they see themselves as having a problem and if so, in what ways do they find it affects them? As these questions are asked and the answers listened to and reflected upon, the client will hopefully begin to recognise that it is *their* feelings and concerns that will be prioritised in the therapy and not anyone else's.

Generally in this introductory session, it is important to explain something of the counselling frame to the client in terms of confidentiality. It is important to let them know that they may disclose anything they like within the session without any fear that it will be shared without their permission. Most importantly, this is an opportunity to explain the limits of confidentiality and let the client know that nothing from the session will be shared unless there is concern that there is a risk of significant harm to them, either from themselves or from another. It is essential to ensure that they have understood what has been said regarding confidentiality and that they consent to those limits. Naturally, this needs to be done in a way which takes into account both chronological age and cognitive capacities for understanding as referred to earlier. The issue of confidentiality will be covered in more depth in subsequent chapters.

Having discussed confidentiality, the next stage might be to introduce the concept of the therapeutic space in a way that will make sense to the child or young person. This might include explaining that the purpose of the meeting is to provide a space to help them explore and understand whatever is causing them difficulties or upset. At this point the client can be invited to tell the therapist about themselves and what they think has brought them here, with a suggestion, if appropriate, that they can talk, draw or use any of the other materials in the room to do so. As this initial session proceeds, the work will continue in accordance with the practitioner's own theoretical basis and clinical practice and the age and individual needs of the child or young person.

Case material: Heather and Conor—Part Three

Following on from their initial meeting, Yasmin brings Conor to Heather's consulting room for the second part of the assessment. Heather observes Conor to be a tall and lean eleven-year-old boy. He appears happy to be coming and makes good eye contact with Heather throughout the session. They agree that Yasmin will accompany them for the first twenty minutes of the session but that then she will wait downstairs while Heather and Conor meet alone. When Conor comes into the room he immediately notices the pile of board games on the shelf and asks if they are for playing with. Heather says that they are and suggests that he might like to choose one to play now. He chooses UNO and they sit down to play. Conor immediately takes charge of dealing the cards and telling mum the rules. Heather observes that Conor seems desperate to win and beat his mum. After they have played for a while Heather looks at the clock and reminds Conor that they agreed that mum would go downstairs at this point. Yasmin gets up to leave and Conor says goodbye, barely glancing up at his mum as he does. When she has left, Heather asks Conor if he knows why mum has brought him here. Conor replies that it is because he is being horrible to mum and because he shouts at her if she says he has to do something he doesn't want to. At this point Heather thinks it is important to speak to Conor about confidentiality. She suggests to him that it might be important, before they begin to think about how he is feeling, that he knows that anything he shares in the session will stay between them with certain limits. Conor agrees to this and begins to talk to Heather about how he has felt since his dad left their home.

At the end of the hour, Heather goes downstairs to the waiting room with Conor and asks Heather to discuss with Conor how they would like to proceed and give her a call when they have decided if they would like to go ahead with the counselling.

Assessment of older children and young people

Recent government guidelines in the UK suggest that children aged twelve or over should be assumed to have the capacity to make their own choices regarding medical or other treatment (HM Government, 2004). Therefore, once a child has reached age twelve and over they will require a different approach at assessment. Children of this age are increasingly likely to be recognised as "Gillick" competent, that is, as having reached a sufficient level of understanding and intelligence to understand what therapy might involve, how they might be helped by it and what it means for their counselling to be confidential.

In Piagetian terms they will be likely to be moving beyond the "concrete operational" stage and into the "formal operational stage" (1964) meaning that they can think in the more abstract or hypothetical ways required by the talking therapies. Confidentiality has a great significance for this age group who are generally in the throes of separation and individuation from the family, necessitating the development of a private life, away from prying eyes of parents. As Marks Mishne (1986) writes:

> Adolescent clients need to be informed of the confidentiality of their communications, and their right to share or withhold as they wish. It is hoped that they will come to see that they will not be seduced or forced into any disclosure. Commonly the resistive adolescent perceives the clinician as the pawn or tool of the parents, engaged to reshape the teenager into the compliant child he or she believes the parent seeks. (Marks Mishne, 1986, p. 35)

Although in private practice it is almost always the case that there will be a parent or other third party paying for the therapy, in terms of the law, any child considered "Gillick" competent has the right to access their own therapy without their parents' or guardians explicit knowledge. It is for individual practitioners to decide how they will make a contract should they be approached by a young person able to fund their own therapy and wishing to do so in confidence, but they should recognise there is no legal reason why this should not be a possibility. Indeed, as far as the therapy is concerned, in the assessment of a client deemed "Gillick" competent, there is no actual ethical need for parental involvement in this part of the process at all and all the information gathering may take place between client and therapist. Parents of "Gillick" competent children can potentially provide any background information regarding their child via a telephone conversation or a questionnaire and don't necessarily need to attend a face-to-face assessment session. In some cases, young people may prefer to come to the assessment with their parent and some absolutely don't. A client potentially deemed as "Gillick" competent may or may not involve their parent in the making of this decision. This may depend upon the developmental stage a young person has reached in regards to their relationship with the parent(s) as shown in table 1.1.

Giving information

If therapy is to be successful then practitioners will need to be able to develop an exclusive therapeutic relationship with their client, supported by the parent(s) or carer. To facilitate this, all parties need clarity and understanding to some degree regarding the nature of the therapeutic relationship. One of the functions of assessment mentioned in Tantam's (1995) paper on the process is that of "information giving" and this can be extremely important when working in this particular context. Even when parents agree in principle to the confidential nature of the counselling relationship they may not have understood fully what this will mean in reality. They may expect when they return to collect their child from the session or when the door to the waiting room opens at ten to four that they will be given a full report on the activities and progress which have taken place. Perhaps they have come to expect this from other professionals in whose care they leave their children, and they may well expect a counsellor to be no different. It can therefore come as a shock when their child is returned to them at the end of the session without an accompanying report. It can leave an unprepared parent feeling anxious and excluded and, if left unaddressed, this can have a negative impact on the progress or even the future of the therapy. As Geldard and Geldard (2002) note:

> It is helpful to warn parents that at times their child may not wish to disclose information arising from a therapy session. It is reasonable to expect that parents may feel anxious and believe that they might be left without information which they should right-fully know. (Geldard & Geldard, 2002, p. 11)

In view of this it can be helpful to discuss with parents before therapy begins how they will manage the sharing of information about sessions. This could be done initially in a conversation during the assessment process and then supported by a written information sheet for parents to take away with them from the assessment and refer to in the future. Some children may wish to share the contents of their sessions with their parents and this is of course up to them. It is most important for parents to be aware that the therapist will not routinely share informa-tion but also that they will not be left uninformed should anything be disclosed in a session which indicates that their child may be in any danger. If explained properly, most parents can understand that their child's counselling must feel safe and exclusive if they are to be able to truly explore issues which they find troubling without fear of paren-tal intrusion or of upsetting an already anxious parent further. With younger children this can be aided by scheduling regular reviews of the counselling when, with the client's permission, appropriate aspects of the work can be shared and the parents can contribute their own obser-vations or concerns to the therapy. With older, post-"Gillick" children it is important again to reassure parents that the confidentiality you agree with their child has limits and that you will not maintain confidentiality if there is a significant risk to their child's safety.

Once information has been given, the child has received a taste of the therapy in the form of the assessment session and the practitioner is satisfied that the referral is appropriate for their practice, the parent(s) and child are advised to discuss how they have found the assess-ment and then decide together how they would like to proceed. If the parent and child decides that they would like the therapy to go ahead then the next stage of agreeing upon the therapeutic contract, which is covered in the next chapter, can begin.

Chapter summary

– Assessment is an important phase of the therapy which can influence greatly the success of the next stage of the work.
– The initial referral is an opportunity to begin to create an alliance with the parent, essential to the success of working with children in private practice.
– Gather as much information as you can about the family and the client's early life.
– Assess where the client is developmentally in relation to their chronological age using appropriate theoretical models before deciding on treatment plan.
– Discuss confidentiality with both client and parent(s) in age and developmentally appropriate ways.

CHAPTER TWO

Contracting and establishing the therapeutic frame

C ontracting and establishing a framework within which therapy can take place are integral parts of the counselling and psychotherapy process. The therapeutic frame allows the therapist to define the therapeutic relationship; its terms and limitations. The therapeutic frame and contract are what differentiate therapy from other kinds of "helping" conversations such as might be had with a friend, a priest or other family member. A thoughtful and well-designed frame for therapy will undoubtedly have a major impact upon the success of the work which takes place within it. Once the frame and contract have been established and agreed upon, both parties can feel safe enough to begin the therapeutic work. The following chapter examines how the contract is important in establishing the frame for therapeutic work with children and young people and where particular care and attention are required due to the complexities of contracting with this group in private practice.

The contract

However the contract or framework for a therapeutic relationship is set out by the practitioner, there will generally be, in private practice at least, some elements of the contract which are negotiated. A practitioner may have already decided that they require a financial payment for their services and that the fee must be paid regardless of whether the client attends their session or not, while some practitioners may allow sessions to be cancelled with a certain amount of notice, or for the day/time to be altered. However flexible or firmly fixed a practitioner's particular therapy contract is, and whatever the theoretical and clinical basis adhered to in setting and maintaining it, there are likely to be elements that are decided with clients on an individual basis. These may be something as relatively straightforward as negotiations regarding the exact amount of fee to be paid. Many practitioners offer a "sliding scale" of fees to accommodate the reality of different incomes and personal circumstances. Frequency of sessions is also something which may be negotiated when contracting as well as whether the therapy will be open-ended or run to a certain number of sessions before review or termination. When working with an adult client in private practice, these negotiations can take place between the client and therapist, generally without the direct involvement of any third party. An adult client can decide for themselves, in conjunction with their therapist, whether open-ended, twice a week therapy would be most helpful for their particular issue and whether this is something they have the necessary resources to commit to, or whether they would prefer or can only realistically embark upon a fixed-term weekly therapy to work on one particular troubling issue. The important point here is that the decision, in part at least, belongs to the client. They may have to consider whether they or the family have the funds to support them, and whether they are able to free up the time from other commitments to attend sessions. However, they also have a great deal of autonomy in choosing the terms of their therapy when compared to children and young people. With clients in this age group, most of these decisions will be made by their parents, or other parties.

For Anna Freud (1965), this presented the child or adolescent therapist with a fundamental difficulty; "Since the child does not enter analysis of his own free will, and makes no contract with the analyst, he does not feel bound by any analytic rules. (A. Freud, 1965, p. 34), suggesting that the act of deciding to enter therapy oneself is a vital component of the therapeutic contract and, without this element, there is a concern that the client has not really themselves entered into and/or fully subjected themselves to the process of analysis. This is an important point

to consider and to be aware of when working therapeutically with this age group who are still, to a greater or lesser extent, dependent upon parent or carers. The dilemma for practitioners here is how to hold in mind and contain the third party in the form of parent or carer while also holding the child in mind as the client.

In practice, this means that in making the therapeutic contract with children and young people, the third party, usually a parent or carer, must be considered. Therapists working with this group in private practice cannot contract exclusively with either client or parent, unless the young person is of "Gillick" competency and able to fund their therapy via independent means. There are clearly the same distinctions between children of different ages and developmental stages as were encountered in the previous chapter on assessment, and a younger child will do less of the contractual negotiating than perhaps will a teenager of fifteen or older. The constant factor here is that the responsibility for payment for the therapy will usually fall upon someone other than the client themselves. This will have an undeniable impact on the process of contracting and carrying out therapeutic work in the context of private practice.

As briefly mentioned in the previous chapter, there are circumstances when a young person either over sixteen or considered "Gillick" competent might request therapy without the financial support or involvement of their parent. In these cases, if a practitioner considered it ethical to do so, they would contract with the client in the same way as they would were they over eighteen. For the purposes of this chapter and the rest of the book as a whole, however, the focus will be on work with children and young people where a third party is paying the fee as this is the most usual circumstance in work with this age group.

Case material: Heather and Conor—Part Four

Yasmin contacts Heather by telephone the day after the assessment with Conor to say that he would like to begin some sessions with Heather as soon as possible. Heather suggests a time later that week to which Yasmin agrees. Heather has already given Yasmin a copy of her therapy contract to look at. They agree that Yasmin will sign it and return it to Heather when she brings Conor in for his session, along with a copy of the referral form, which includes a space for Yasmin to confirm that she gives parental consent for the counselling to take place. They agree the fee that Yasmin will pay for the sessions and Yasmin says that she intends to speak to Conor's dad about sharing the cost of the counselling but she is not sure he will be willing to do so. They also agree that they will review Conor's counselling together after six sessions. Heather reminds Yasmin that she will not be able to share any information about the content of Conor's sessions with her and that what is shared at the review will only be what Conor is happy for his mum to be aware of. She advises that they will wait until nearer the time to see what form the review will take and who will be involved in it. Yasmin is happy with all of this and agrees that the counselling needs to feel like a safe space for Conor to be able to open up in. She ends the conversation saying that she just wants her happy little boy back again.

The fee

For the most part in therapy for this age group it is the parent or carer who pays the fee for the therapy sessions and who is therefore making a financial investment in the process. This leads to an important question for practitioners regarding the meaning of this investment and who has "ownership" of the sessions and sets the agenda; client or parent?

Fee is a vital element of the frame in adult counselling and psychotherapy. When a practitioner sets a fee with their client they are asking them to invest in and commit to the therapy, as well as introducing an element of reality into the process regarding their own needs, including that of needing to earn a living. Anne Gray (1994) argues in her book *An Introduction to the Therapeutic Frame*, that the fee, along with other aspects of the therapeutic contract represents Freud's "reality principle" (1920) in action;

> The reality is that therapists have needs of their own: they have to earn money in order to live; they have interests outside the therapeutic encounter; they have other clients; they need rest and relief- just as parents have needs of their own which may conflict with the needs of an individual child. (Gray, 1994, p. 11)

In *Money Matters: The Fee in Psychotherapy and Psychoanalysis*, Herron and Welt (1992) argue further to this that the fee is a taboo subject for most therapists who feel guilt for inflicting the demand of a payment on their client. The therapist's "love" and regard for their client is not unconditional and this is demonstrated primarily via the fee charged for the session and therefore for the therapist's time and concern. They argue that this difficulty with the fee still exists in therapeutic relationships where the fee is not directly paid by the client;

> In some instances the payment may be made by a parent or a spouse. Still, the patient pays because the people putting up the money expect payment of some kind—gratitude, understanding, changed attitudes—from the patient. The transaction between patient and therapist is more remote, but the payment concept is constant. Furthermore, the people paying the money may well expect an accounting from the therapists. (Herron & Welt, 1992, p. 6)

It is these expectations of payment in kind, identified here by Herron and Welt (1992) that therapists need to be aware of when working with the client and parent at the same time. When a parent brings their child for therapy, they may often have a clear idea themselves of what their child's "problem" is as well as what needs to be done to "solve" it. For example, the parents of a child with issues around eating may bring their child expecting the therapist to help their child to start eating "normally" again and gaining weight. They are expecting a change of attitude, and concern for their child means that they are hoping it will happen fast. Facilitating their child eating normally and gaining weight will most likely be the priority and often the only concern for parents. Their agenda when contracting is clear; I am paying you to use your expertise to get my child to begin eating "normally" again. Practitioners may well find themselves wanting to take a different approach to setting an agenda for the therapy, taking into account the experience of the client and an attempt, for example, to understand the underlying communication beneath the eating behaviour as a method of helping the client to regain a healthy relationship with food. Clearly, in the example of a client who is becoming anorexic and losing significant amounts of weight rapidly, it may be vital to increase their calorific intake quickly in order to reduce the risk of cognitive impairment and harm to the body and vital organs. Working with young people where eating has become severely disordered will be covered in more depth in the chapter on working with risk further on in this book.

Similarly, if a child's "bad" behaviour is causing distress to a parent it may be this which prompts them to look for counselling for them. This behaviour could be anything including self-harm and injury, substance misuse, or angry outbursts of shouting and swearing at their parent. Once again, the fact that the parent is paying for the session may mean that they believe, either consciously or unconsciously, that the therapeutic outcome is theirs and that therefore they should be allowed to decide what the objective of the therapy should be. They may feel frustrated when the therapist does not join with them in condemning their child's behaviour and setting about to bring it into line, but instead makes an attempt to understand and help the child communicate their feelings in a more appropriate and healthy manner.

It may be very useful for practitioners to bear in mind that the fee in child and adolescent therapy represents a monetary exchange for the skills and expertise of the professional in working with the issues as presented by the client, rather than "ownership" of the therapeutic process and its outcome. It is important that practitioners are clear about this in their own minds when they embark on work in this field as this will allow them to retain clarity regarding their role.

Just as with adult clients paying for their own therapy, a parent paying for private therapy for their child cannot necessarily buy a particular therapeutic outcome, but they certainly can negotiate in terms of how much they are willing to pay and for how long. Since for the most part therapy in private practice does involve a direct financial transaction, the person at the paying end of that transaction holds significant power in terms of being able to decide whether or not they continue to pay for the service. For some parents this may relate to their own financial realities, although it may also reflect their need to maintain some control of the therapeutic process. Private counselling or psychotherapy is a relatively expensive regular commitment, and for some parents, however concerned they are for their child's wellbeing and invested in helping them, they may not have the available funds to pay a fee indefinitely. This leads us to another important aspect of the therapeutic frame; establishment of therapeutic goals and length of contract.

Establishing goals for therapy

Before thinking more specifically about how long to contract to work with a client there must first be some consideration of what the goals or aims are for therapy. It may be that these have been fairly clear from the time of the initial referral. At their first contact with the therapist, the parent(s) may have a goal or goals in mind, which were then confirmed during the assessment process. For example, a parent may be looking for resolution of a specific symptomatic or behavioural issue which is troubling them or their child. It may be apparent to the therapist from the assessment process that the child is dealing with issues relating to a specific source of distress, for example, parental separation, loss of a parent through death or divorce, illness etc. and that the therapeutic work will be focussed on helping them to come to terms with this issue and find new ways of managing which are less distressing for themselves and their family. If the child is generally developing well apart from the issues which have arisen and they have an adequate support structure around them, it may be that a satisfactory therapeutic outcome can be achieved within a relatively few sessions. In this situation it can be useful to discuss with the parent(s) a contract for a specific number of sessions, and then have a review session of some kind to establish if the therapeutic goal is on course to be achieved. This type of flexible and adaptive structure allows the practitioner to develop the therapy from the assessment onwards, according to the needs of the client. First, an assessment is offered (A), followed by a fixed number of sessions (S), then a review (R), and then either an ending phase consisting of a fixed number of sessions focussing on termination and bringing the work to a conclusion (E) or further sessions and/or reviews. The following are examples of how this might look in practice:

$$A + 6S + R + 2E \quad \text{or} \quad A + 6S + R + 4S + 2E$$

The flexibility of this structure works well when practitioners find that further issues emerge as the therapy proceeds potentially requiring additional sessions. During the review which could take place by phone or in person, both with and without the client present depending on what is appropriate in individual cases, these additional issues can be discussed fully and a decision made as to how to work with them. It may be decided the most benefit will be gained by staying focussed on the original therapeutic work and to perhaps treat the emerging issues separately at a different time. This review can also be an opportunity to discuss any issues arising from the therapy that indicate the client could need to be referred onto another service, or that work with other family members would be useful. These processes will be discussed in depth in later chapters.

Therapeutic goals and length of contract can also be less simple to negotiate than as outlined in the above. Parents do not always refer their children with issues which are arising from such definite issues. Often issues and problems have existed for a long time and it is only when a crisis occurs that children are referred for therapy.

Competing agendas

Therapeutic work with children and adolescents really requires therapists to think collaboratively with clients and parents to set realistic goals for the therapy. How these goals are set and what they constitute will be influenced considerably by several factors; the age and developmental stage a client has reached; their psychological mindedness or ego-functioning; the conditions they are living in, that is, whether they are well supported socially etc.; whether the work is intended to be brief or open-ended and the theoretical model used by the therapist.

In *Counselling Children* (2002), Geldard and Geldard set out four levels of goals in working therapeutically with children. These are:

    Level 1 goals—fundamental goals
    Level 2 goals—the parents' goals
    Level 3 goals—goals formulated by the counsellor
    Level 4 goals—the child's goals. (Geldard & Geldard, 2002, p. 6)

Considering different "levels" of goals in this way allows the practitioner to see clearly where one agenda for the therapy could dominate the goal setting process, potentially effecting the ethical basis, and the positive outcome of the work. For example, if only the parents' goals are taken into consideration, then the practitioner may lose sight of what the child as client would like from their counselling, potentially resulting in the client feeling uninvolved in the therapy and unable to benefit from it. Alternatively, if the parent's goals are not taken into consideration, they may decide that their child's best interest is not being appropriately considered and that there is nothing to be gained from them investing in the therapy, and withdraw their support for the process.

Practitioners themselves will have their own fundamental therapeutic aims, largely consistent across all the therapeutic work they undertake with clients. These may include aims such as improving the client's ability to deal with emotional difficulties, raising their self-esteem, enabling them to manage their feelings and behaviours so they don't experience excessive negative consequences, amongst others. These aims are largely influenced and supported by the ethical basis of therapeutic work. An example is the principle of "beneficence", as proposed by BACP (British Association for Counselling and Psychotherapy) (2013) ethical framework, which requires practitioners to always ensure that the work they are doing is of benefit to their client. Beneficence is a useful principle to have in mind in the complexity of working with children, as it allows the therapist to always remember that the child is the client and not the parent, and any therapy must be of benefit to the child before the parent.

The fundamental aim of therapy, to improve emotional and psychological wellbeing and increase a client's ability to engage positively with their own life and the lives of others, must be at the heart of all therapeutic endeavour, and form the bedrock from which all other goals will be formed, regardless of individual theoretical or clinical models. The work of therapy, whether with children or adults, is to understand what impedes a client's ability and functioning in these areas and then to try to address these factors.

Parental goals for therapy may be very specific, and are often related to their own agenda for their children. This is exemplified in the case material at the start of the chapter when Conor's mum says to Heather that she just wants her "happy little boy" back. Parents referring their children for therapy in private practice will do so generally because they have identified something about their child's behaviour, or wellbeing, as dysfunctional or distressing in some way, and have been advised, or come to the conclusion themselves that this can best be dealt with in therapy. As discussed briefly in the chapter on assessment, parents come to therapy for their children with varying degrees of understanding regarding how the difficulties have arisen, and often with differing ideas about how they might be addressed. Many parents understandably hold out the hope that therapy will provide some sort of magic "fix" for their child so that the troubling symptoms will disappear and may be disappointed when this does not prove to be the case.

With young children, the parental agenda for therapeutic goals can have more significance in work than with older children. Prior to puberty and the beginning of adolescence, children are unlikely to voice their own desire for therapy themselves. It is parents, or possible teachers or other adults with whom they are in contact, who will identify a problem and then refer the child either to their GP, or directly to a therapist. In this respect, the parent's agenda is vital, as without their concerns the child would not enter or continue in therapy at all. The child's goals, prior to adolescence are much harder to ascertain than the parent's and even the therapist's. Practitioners must observe closely the material the client brings to each session, particularly early on, and then use these observations to ascertain what they need from their therapy and therefore what goals to set.

Case Material: Heather and Conor—Part Five

> Heather and Conor meet for their first appointment, Heather having contracted with Yasmin that they will have six sessions before reviewing the counselling. Initially Heather reiterates the agreement around confidentiality and explains to Conor that they now have six sessions together before they consider if they need more or whether they can bring the counselling to a close. Heather lets Conor know that they have forty minutes together and that he can choose how to use that time. They can talk, or he can use any of the other materials in the room. Heather explains that hopefully the sessions will help them to get to the bottom of whatever has been bothering Conor and preventing him from enjoying his activities.

The case material above demonstrates how the counsellor's agenda, and the parent's agenda at this point are the most significant in the work. Yasmin has stated that she has noticed that Conor is not enjoying activities that were previously important to him and Heather indicates to Conor that one of the goals of the therapy will be to understand what has caused this change. Heather's hope at this point is that the reasons why this change has occurred and Conor's own feelings about it will emerge in the course of the therapy in a way that allows them to work on them together.

Establishing goals—adolescents and young people

As previously discussed, contracting and goal setting with adolescents and young people can be less straightforward than with younger children, particularly due to the circumstances of adolescence. During this phase, as we know, young people are beginning to do the important work of separation and individuation from their parents and attempting to establish a separate identity of their own. Adolescence can be seen as a phase of mourning the childhood attachments to mum and dad, as well as movement towards establishing new attachments outside of the family environment. During adolescence, young people are naturally less compliant with their parents' ideas of appropriate behaviour and what constitutes dysfunctional choices and methods of managing emotions. This is shown in the following case example:

> The mother of a sixteen-year-old boy, Louis, contacts a child psychotherapist regarding concerns about her son's use of cannabis and frequent angry outbursts. In an initial phone consultation with the therapist, his mother says that her son's use of cannabis is "excessive" and she feels strongly that he must stop using drugs altogether. Louis comes reluctantly to his first session where the therapist states that the session is for him to use to talk about whatever he likes. Confidentiality is discussed and the limits agreed upon including what will happen should the therapist feel that Louis is at risk in any respect. Louis says that he knows his mum thinks his drug use is the problem, but as far as he is concerned and, by comparison with friends, his use of cannabis is not excessive, or problematic. He likes to smoke socially as it makes him feel part of the group and accepted by his friends. Louis says that he does not like to drink or hang out with others who use alcohol as he has experienced them as aggressive and volatile, and that he therefore finds smoking cannabis to be "better" for him than the alcohol used by some of his peers.

At this point in the therapy, his mother's goal for the therapy is clearly for Louis to stop using drugs absolutely, as she is making an assumption based on her own knowledge and experience that this is a behaviour which is harmful and dangerous for her son to be engaged in. This may or may not be a correct assumption on her part, but as Louis does not see this as an issue at this stage, to continue with a therapeutic goal of curtailing drug use in line with the parental goal would be to alienate Louis from his own therapy. Here it is important to hold in mind that the therapist's goal might be to help Louis understand his relationship with drugs as well as his relationships with his peers, and then decide for himself whether his use is problematic for him. It may be important for the therapist to help Louis to understand that it may take some time for him to recognise what, if any, goals he might have for his therapy, but that the space is available for him to explore this with the therapist alongside him.

It is especially important for therapists of older children and adolescents to maintain an attitude of curiosity and non-judgement. If this is not the case it may prove difficult for the young person to make effective use of the therapist and the therapy, and there is a danger they will quickly disengage. For many young people, emotional and psychological difficulties arise at a point when their energies are moving away from establishing attachments with adult or parent figures and towards peer group connections. However, since adolescents and young people are also looking for ways of understanding and coming to terms with their rapidly changing selves they often welcome the opportunity to do this alongside someone who is able to support them in this endeavour without prejudice or anxiety of their own.

When goal setting for therapy with adolescents, practitioners must hold a careful balance in terms of ensuring client autonomy while bearing in mind the concerns of the parents as referrers. Practitioners also need to bear in mind that the life aims and objectives of young people going through adolescence will not be the same as those of adult clients. It is not necessarily appropriate for young people in current times to be seeking to be settled and fulfilled in love and work as older adult clients may be striving for as their ultimate goal of therapy. Some degree of risk-taking is a natural part of the life of the adolescent and not necessarily to be seen as undesirable.

For practitioners working with clients of this age group an experience of exploring their own adolescence in personal therapy can be of enormous benefit to their clinical practice. This exploration can enable therapists to be aware of how they themselves negotiated this period and have a sense of their own process in this respect, helping them to maintain separation when encountering the client's own adolescence.

Reviewing progress

Reviews are an integral part of this therapeutic work, offering an opportunity for all parties involved in the therapeutic process to connect and communicate about it and contribute to its onward progress. If clear boundaries have been set-up around the therapy in terms of confidentiality at the beginning and communicated to all parties it should be possible to offer a review which takes into account the concerns and feedback of all while maintaining the needs of the client and the confidentiality of the therapy as paramount.

With younger children the review may take place with the child and parents together or the practitioner may wish to meet with the parents alone for part or all of the session. If the meeting takes place with parent(s) alone there will need to be a conversation with the client beforehand explaining the purpose of the review, and making an agreement together regarding what is ok to for the therapist to share with their parents. This is also an opportunity to review with the client and find out how they are experiencing their therapy and what, if anything, they would like to be different. For the parents, the review is an opportunity for them to comment on any changes they have noticed since the therapy began as well as to raise any further concerns that may have arisen for them. This can also be an opportunity for the practitioner to make further investigations into the client's background and history if there are questions about this which have come up during the course of the therapy. At this point, discussions can take place regarding the possibility of any additional referrals, or family work. This is also the time, if appropriate, to come to an agreement for the therapy to begin moving toward the end-phase.

Just as with the initial assessment, parents can feel extremely anxious when they are coming to the review session. They may have fears that during the course of the therapy their shortcomings or mistakes have emerged, and that they will now be blamed and held to account for all they have done "wrong". When meeting with a client's parent(s) it can be very useful to be mindful of these fears, and aim to create an open and collaborative space where all parties can think and reflect together on how best to assist the client. It may not always be possible to prevent a parent from feeling attacked and becoming defensive during the course of the review, but if care and attention has gone in to setting the frame for the review, just as with a therapy session, then there is more potential for keeping the meeting as constructive as possible. It can help to be open with parents about this from the start and ask them how they are feeling regarding the review and the therapy in general. This allows them to feel acknowledged and valued and can provide beneficial information about how the therapy is currently regarded by the family. If parents are put at their ease initially it can be much easier to cope further on if the session becomes more challenging.

Reviewing work with adolescents and young people

When we are working with an older child or young person the review process is still an important part of the therapy for the reasons mentioned previously, that is, to bring the various parties together in order to provide feedback and make decisions regarding the future of the work. With this particular group it may not be appropriate or necessary to have parent(s) attend in person for a review session although equally this may be something that the young person wishes to take place.

If appropriate the review can take place over the phone, and may consist of an agreement around continuing sessions or bringing them to a close. Parents of adolescents and young people can occupy various positions in relation to their child's therapy and these are useful for practitioners to observe and take note of. The way a parent treats their involvement in their child's therapy can provide important information about their relationship in general with the life of their child. Some parents and carers remain very much in the background of their child's therapy throughout the process. This may be because they see their child at this stage as having a more or less separate life from them, and their respect for this means they would not want to intrude upon their therapy out of respect for their child's privacy. These parents may recognise they have a part to play in their still partially dependent child's life, and they are happy to support the work financially, or in any other respect if required. On other occasions, a parent's detachment could be indicative of a general neglect and lack of interest in their child's life beyond the willingness to pay for sessions to continue. In this respect similar behaviour by a parent can indicate very different family dynamics.

There are, however, some parents who take up a far more active role in relation to their child's therapy and, once again, this can be indicative of the family dynamics. It can be important when reviewing the work with a parent who is very interested in the therapy to be sure that they understand the boundaries of confidentiality and are clear as to what their role is in respect of the review. Practitioners have a vital role to play in this respect and this is another area of the work which can be quite tricky to negotiate. Parents may come to the review with increasing areas of their child's life which they feel anxious about and want addressed in the therapy sessions with their child. They may be concerned about drug use or self-harm, or about the way their child speaks or behaves towards them between sessions. When such issues arise during contact with parents, it can be easy for the therapist to feel that they must try to address these concerns, regardless of their therapeutic relevance, in order not to disappoint the parent and therefore potentially put the survival of the therapy at risk. Parents can feel extremely worried about their child's behaviour, and may want their concerns addressed and anxiety lessened. The key point to remember is that the parents' anxiety is not the main focus or concern of the therapy. The primary consideration must always be the client themselves and, while parents can be sympathised with in terms of the difficulties they are going through, they may also need gentle encouragement to find support for themselves with this elsewhere. This may be in their own therapy, support groups, or in their network of family and friends. Parents may be greatly helped when a practitioner acknowledges how much anxiety can be raised by having a child going through therapy, and how difficult it might feel for them to be on their own with this. Some parents do not have a good support network, or they may not feel able to discuss their child's therapy with close family or friends, and therefore may find the offer of alternative therapeutic support most useful.

As adults and sometimes parents themselves, practitioners may find it hard to resist the seduction of helping parents to manage their anxiety, when it is the child whom they have been contracted to help. The therapist may well experience a natural identification with the plight of a mother or father who feels helpless in the face of their teen's distressing behaviour and who look to them for help and reassurance. Therapists working with this age group are likely to be closer in age to the parent than to the client, and may even have similar concerns about their own children. These factors can add to the difficulty in holding clearly in mind who the client is, and what the therapeutic work is, in this case. In this respect, clinical supervision provides an essential space for the therapist to reflect on these conflicts should they arise, and find the means to manage them in the therapeutic process.

Feelings of envy may also arise in the relationship between therapist and parent. Parents may see the therapist as having taken on the role of confidante for their child, usually a position they themselves have held until recently in the case of an adolescent or older child. They may feel envious of the perceived closeness between the therapist and their child, or of the therapist's apparent skill in helping their child where they perceive themselves as having failed. It can also be painful for parents when therapists are not prepared to share their child's confidences with them in order to make up for their loss in this respect.

In work with adolescents, the review may also be an opportunity, where it is in the client's best interest and agreed to by them, for a family session involving parents and client in order to open up a conversation about how to best support their child within the family dynamic. During the course of the therapy, an understanding may develop regarding the ways in which the client experiences the home environment as contributing to their issues. The review can be a facilitative space where different viewpoints can be expressed, and all voices heard. This kind of review will be discussed further in the chapter on working with other family members.

Breaks in the therapy

Breaks are a significant part of therapeutic work in private practice in work with children and young people. Therapists often have an established practice around contracting for breaks and holidays with adult clients which may need to be adapted for work with a different client group. With younger children, who are dependent upon their parents to bring them to and from their therapy sessions, the therapy can quickly become part of the family routine. It is important to bear in mind that often this routine is very much connected to school term times, and it can become harder to manage sessions during the school holidays. This is where flexibility with regards to individual clients, and their situations is necessary. For some children, attendance outside of term time can become quite difficult and, if appropriate to the work, it can be useful at times to see the school holidays as providing natural breaks between pieces of work, as in school counselling. It is worth noting that this may mean that child client breaks may not completely coincide with a practitioners planned breaks from adult work, and this is something for practitioners to take into account when making plans regarding projected income, or fees charged. With some children, breaks around the school holidays may not be necessary or desirable. It may be necessary to keep the momentum of the work going, and both client and parent may be fully committed to continuing the therapy inside and out of term time.

With older adolescents and young people who are still at school or college, attendance outside of term time can, again, be problematic. For many young people beginning to gain independence and autonomy about how they spend their time, the holidays can feel like their time to do with what they want, as oppose to the rigid constraints of term-time and the school or college timetable. If there is a sense with a particular client that this is the case, it may be more beneficial for the client to have a break from the therapy while they are out of school than to ask them to continue to attend, something they may experience as punitive and authoritarian. It can of course also be useful to explore these issues with our young clients. How does it feel for them to continue to attend their sessions when they would rather be on the beach or playing football? It is important for therapists to be sensitive to the difference between times when holding clients in such an exploration is useful and productive, and when it becomes potentially damaging for the therapeutic alliance. The attitude of the therapist here is vital in conveying to the adolescent client that their need for the therapy can be held in mind, as well as their need for separation. The provision of a therapeutic frame which is consistent and structured enough to provide stability and tolerable levels of frustration for clients, along with the flexibility to allow them the freedom to move away and then re-engage with sessions when the break comes to an end, can be most useful in this respect.

Endings

Endings are a big part of therapeutic work and need to be held in mind from the very beginning within the contract. As part of the therapy contract it is usual to talk about the process of ending and there is much in the therapeutic literature (Edwards, 1997), regarding the termination process in therapy as well as unplanned endings and ambivalence from both client and therapist when it comes to bringing the work and the relationship to a close.

With younger children the end will usually be agreed upon by both the client, parents, and practitioner together. Ideally this will happen because a satisfactory point has been reached in the work where the client and family feel they have gained enough from the therapy process to be able to continue to move forward independently, without regular sessions. A plan may be negotiated in the ending phase to include follow-up sessions in the future to review progress following termination, or it may be agreed that the family will make contact themselves should further work be considered necessary. This will all depend very much upon how the family have found the therapy, as well as on the original presenting concerns.

There is much to be found in the literature around work with adolescents regarding the infrequency with which their therapy is brought to a satisfactory conclusion. It can be true that young people can be less willing to complete either "working through", or termination phases. Some theorists (Coren, 1996; Shefler, 2000), have suggested that for this reason, brief therapeutic interventions are more suited to those going through the adolescent stage. Shefler (2000) notes; "Many adolescents in need of therapy resist long-term attachment and involvement in an ambiguous relationship, which they experience as a threat to their emerging sense of independence and separateness" (Shefler, 2000, p. 88). It might be helpful to think of therapy with adolescents and young people as a little like a picnic. The therapist offers a space, sets out the food on a blanket and then allows the young person to interact with this in whatever way they need within the structure provided. It can be the mark of a successful picnic when a young person is able to sit down to eat and then get up and go off re-engage with friends or other aspects of their life when they have had what they needed. They may not want or be able to stay and talk about how it feels to be leaving the picnic. They know on some level that they can't stay in therapy forever, but they may also not want to say goodbye completely. To return to the picnic analogy, if they say goodbye properly you may think that they won't be hungry again and pack everything away. Many young people want to leave the therapy for now, but need to know that you, or another like you, will be available should they need to return at some point. The challenge here for therapists is to let go of some of the traditional ideas they may hold regarding the importance of working through, and coming to a point of termination, and offer flexibility to young clients, while maintaining boundaries, and challenging acting out where necessary.

Summary
<ul><li>The therapy contract is an integral part of all counselling and psycho-therapy work.</li><li>In this area of work, the contract is often negotiated between therapist, client, and parent(s)/carer.</li><li>Goal setting for the therapy takes place on a variety of levels. The needs of the client must be paramount.</li><li>Therapeutic goal setting needs to be flexible to take into account the developmental stage of the client.</li><li>Reviews are an opportunity to look at the progress of the therapy and receive feedback from all parties involved.</li><li>Breaks and endings need to be discussed with all parties. Clients are encouraged to end the work with the therapist where possible although individual needs will be taken into account.</li></ul>

CHAPTER THREE

Setting up: creating a setting for therapy with children and young people

Practicalities: the room

As with all aspects of the therapeutic process, the physical setting in which it takes place will have an undoubted impact on the therapy and needs careful consideration. For Langs (1998);

> The setting is the consistent and reliable backdrop or stage for the unfolding of the therapy. It is an essential part of the therapist's hold and containment of, and adaptation to, the patient. The setting reflects the extent of the therapist's consistency and stability, and his or her preferred means of coping with adaptation- evoking, emotionally charged triggering events. (Langs, 1998, p. 111)

Langs places great emphasis on the impact of the setting on the therapeutic process which will unfold within it. This impact could, arguably, be even greater when the clients are children and young people entering the unfamiliar world of therapy, whether it is taking place in a therapist's home or clinic setting.

It may appear initially that a therapist has few practical and material needs when it comes to setting up in practice. The basic requirements

45

are a room which has good enough soundproofing and a door which closes securely and will not be opened without invitation. These are necessary in order to ensure, as far as is possible, the confidentiality of the session contents. Inside the room itself, most therapists will place a box of tissues within easy reach of the client, in order to convey something of the idea that clients are welcome to let their emotions out in this space and that they can be contained. There will also be some kind of clock, so that the therapist can manage the time boundaries of the session. Seating is another essential and, whether chairs or a couch are being used, they must allow therapist and client to be seated in relative comfort while the therapeutic work takes place. This basic set-up lays the material foundations for the establishment of the therapeutic frame and the beginning of therapeutic work. These essential furnishings, which will vary considerably according to the taste of individual clinicians or those providing therapy rooms for hire, are intended to convey an atmosphere of safety and comfort where, the hope is, deep emotions and thoughts can be encountered and explored within the boundary of the therapeutic hour. Clearly there are many variations on this basic set-up and some methods of therapeutic intervention will require different elements, especially when work takes place remotely over the internet. The BACP has produced a useful and comprehensive information sheet on this subject for their members entitled "Setting up a therapy room", details of which are included in the useful resources section of this book.

When a practitioner intends to open up their practice and premises to children and young people, it is important that they consider the nature of the work to be undertaken and what, if any, changes are required to any basic set-up already in place in order to facilitate this transition.

Clearly the fundamental elements outlined above remain as relevant to work with children and young people as they are to adult therapy. A space is needed for children and young people which is safe, comfortable, and welcoming. For some young people this need may be met by the kind of space we offer to adult clients, but younger children and teenagers may have different needs. For children, a room furnished with large adult-sized chairs and neutral decor may not feel like "their" kind of place. It may be experienced as intimidating or belonging to the unfamiliar world of "grown-ups", where they are perhaps unlikely to be understood or sympathised with. If there is nothing in the room but chairs and tissues and a clock, a child may feel under pressure to maintain eye contact and talk with an adult with whom they are unfamiliar, in a situation about which they may feel understandable anxiety. Sometimes the pervading "adult" atmosphere in a counselling room can be neutralised well enough by the addition of objects or therapeutic materials which might be more familiar to children and help them to feel that this is a space where they might feel more able to relax and express themselves. Coloured cushions or beanbags can be used to some effect along with the provision of various basic art materials, such as felt-tip pens and paper. Bowls or boxes containing small toy animals and other toys and figures can be set out before the session, conveying to younger clients that this is somewhere where play and creativity is welcomed and accommodated.

Practitioners can, of course, go as far with this as they like or the limits of the setting allow. If a therapist is likely to be changing the purpose of their room from adult to child clients and then back again several times in a day according to their appointment diary they are unlikely to be able to provide a traditional "play therapy" environment with dolls house and paint and other creative materials. However, this should not preclude anyone from working with children or being able to provide a space in which they will feel comfortable, welcomed, and accommodated with relatively little material change to the existing room.

Toys and play

Whatever a practitioner's theoretical orientation or their chosen method of working and understanding children and young people, play and art in some form can be a vital part of both establishing the therapeutic alliance and the therapeutic work itself with this group. Many of the major theorists on child counselling and therapy have written extensively on the importance of play for children in therapy and on how the child's inner world can often be understood and reached by observing closely their interaction with toys, sand, and art materials (Axline, 1947; Oaklander, 1978). Although it is beyond the scope of this book to go further into the subject of play and art therapy, it is useful for the practitioner wishing to work with children to do so themselves and there are many books and training courses on this subject readily available.

Practicalities: scheduling appointments

Thinking about possibly adapting the therapeutic space for children and young people raises the question of scheduling appointments for children and young people. As mentioned above, rapid changes in consulting room use from work with children to seeing adults and young people can mean a lot of changes to the layout and/or contents of the space and may also ask a lot of the therapist themselves in terms of changing their way of working throughout the day. Some practitioners may be happy to have play and art equipment visible throughout their day, regardless of whether they are working with children or adult clients and, equally, some therapists may use creative materials irrespective of whether they are seeing children or adults. Some practitioners may choose to try to divide their week or day up into times when they will work with younger children, and times with adults or young people. This can simplify things a great deal in terms of having a full day when the space is dedicated to work with children and all the art and play equipment can remain out and the appropriate seating in use. Although this kind of division of time is not always possible when practitioners have to schedule according to the availability of busy families and clients it is worth bearing in mind. If practitioners are fortunate enough to have access to more than one room it might be possible to have one permanently set-up to accommodate work with children and teenagers. If it is possible to devote a space permanently to therapeutic work with children and young people practitioners may want to go much further with the inclusion of materials and equipment for play and creative interventions. If paint and clay are to be used then access to a sink is important. A doll's house is a useful addition to a play therapy room, as are sand and puppets.

Duration of sessions and time in between

When thinking about scheduling appointments, it is also important to consider what the duration of sessions will be as well as whether extra time will be required in between sessions for clearing up and writing up notes. There is some benefit in being flexible as far as session duration is concerned. Younger children are unlikely to be able to manage a full fifty minute session and therefore it can be useful to accommodate this with flexibility around session length. When meeting the child or young person for the assessment session it may be possible to gauge at this point what they are likely to be able to manage in terms of session duration, although this can also be adjusted once the therapy is in progress.

Even if a therapist is not working strictly as a play or art therapist, and even if clients do not engage with the creative materials provided, simply by providing them the practitioner will have begun the work by demonstrating that they are willing to have the client's needs in mind. Children and young people may find the intensity of a forty or fifty minute session quite anxiety raising. If they are provided with pens and paper or objects to fiddle with, this gives them something to focus on when they are finding talking or even eye contact difficult to maintain. Again, this is not about a play therapy intervention, but about how the environment provided for younger clients will differ from that provided for adults in recognition of their differing needs.

Premises

Therapists in private practice see their clients in a variety of settings such as a dedicated clinic, converted building, or their own homes. Practitioners working at home, or in a rented space or office away from home, must be aware of and adhere to all health and safety guidance relevant to the setting in which they work. Bond and Mitchels (2011) provide useful guidance for therapists in this respect in their book *Legal Issues Across Counselling and Psychotherapy Settings* in the chapter relating to private practice.

Waiting room

The waiting room holds a position of particular importance in work with children and young people and represents to some extent a part of the therapeutic frame, with both its use and meaning varying enormously from child to child and family to family. In practical terms, younger clients are more likely to be accompanied to their session than older or adult clients and a waiting room of some sort is very useful in this respect. The waiting room can represent a transitional space where the therapist comes to meet their client for the first time and where they will be collected from and returned to in subsequent sessions. Younger children and those who are more anxious, particularly at the start of their therapy, may be very pleased to know that their parent is in the waiting room within reach, and may therefore find it easier to relax into their session and the therapeutic relationship. Ideally, the waiting room or space will be in close enough proximity to the therapy room to maintain a sense of the parents' presence but separate enough to ensure the content of the session remains confidential. For parents too, the provision of a waiting room such as this can help them to feel, to some extent, "part of" the therapy while remaining outside the room itself. This can be very important in establishing an exclusive therapeutic relationship with the client which the parent is nonetheless an important part of.

For older children and adolescents the waiting room may have different significance. If their parents wait for them while they are in their session it might be important to gain a sense of how they experience their presence. Some young people may feel that this is an attempt by the parent to intrude into their space, triggering angry feelings. Others may use it as a way of speaking loudly in the sessions of anger towards their parent in the hope that they might be heard. Often therapeutic work with adolescent clients centres on issues of separation and individuation, and parental behaviour around the waiting room with this age group can tell us much about the dynamics in the family regarding separation. While some parents seem unable to imagine not remaining close by throughout their child's session, there are others who seem unable to stay at all. It can also be interesting and valuable to the work to observe parents who seem anxious to drop their child at the door and disappear for some snatched "me time" or those children who arrive in a taxi and then sit in the waiting room alone at the end of the session waiting for another to collect them. In child and adolescent work in particular, the waiting room becomes a part of the therapeutic frame which involves others in relation to the client and therefore is of enormous interest to the therapist attempting to gain a sense of a client via this little window into family dynamics.

Boundaries

The therapy waiting room can come to represent a powerful transitional space for clients, between their inner and outer worlds and their shifting identity as both individuals in their own right and as part of the family. It is therefore important that therapists bear this in mind when managing the boundaries around the waiting area. Whereas the boundaries regarding the actual therapy session itself may seem clear with regards to parents, these can seem less clear in the somewhat less "boundaried" waiting area. On the whole, it is better for practitioners to keep contact with parents in the waiting room to an absolute minimum. Younger children may need to be taken down at the end of their session but this should not then be allowed to become an opportunity for a conversation with the parent to take place. Older children who are happy to do so should be encouraged to leave the session and return to the waiting room on their own. As discussed in a previous chapter, all arrangements for payment are best managed outside of the session, as is any necessary conversation regarding arrangements or changes. Parents may find this somewhat difficult at first, but it is a vital part of establishing trust with the client and enabling them to feel that their therapy belongs to them and that their parent will not be permitted to intrude into their space.

For practitioners working with young children it may be useful to make a policy regarding parental presence on the premises during sessions. If parents plan to leave the premises during their child's session it is also important to make sure that they are aware that they are responsible for their child once the session has ended, and arrangements for their collection need to be solid. Practitioners may decide to stipulate that parents of children under a certain age, for example eleven or twelve, need to stay on the premises during the session. This may be of particular importance for therapists who work in a setting where the waiting room is accessible by members of the public and therefore a child's safety cannot be guaranteed if they are waiting alone for a parent to collect them. This kind of policy and the way in which it is presented to parents can be adapted for the particular setting in which a practitioner is working. It can be very tricky when one young client has not been collected from the waiting area on time and the therapist has another client due.

Setting-up—administration

In terms of record keeping, requirements are much the same as for adult work. Practitioners must ensure their record keeping complies with the requirements of their professional body and with regulations regarding data protection. See further resources section for more information on this. When working with children aged sixteen and under it may be advisable for practitioners to keep a record of written parental permission for the therapy to take place. In the case of divorced or separated parents in the UK only one parent with parental responsibility is required to give permission for therapy. Bond and Mitchels (2011) outline in detail the sometimes complex area of parental responsibility and how it may relate to therapy. Where a child is aged sixteen or over or is deemed to be "Gillick" competent they can consent to their own therapy and no other parental consent is required.

Disclosure and Barring Service
(DBS—formerly "CRB" check)

Counsellors and therapists who work in agency settings whether in a paid or voluntary capacity will have been required to go through a check of their criminal record in order to establish any relevant criminal record they may have and to make sure they do not appear on any lists of those deemed by the relevant authorities to be unsuitable to work with children or the vulnerable. Currently these checks in the UK are carried out by the Disclosure and Barring Service (England and Wales), Disclosure Scotland (Scotland), and Access NI (Northern Ireland). For practitioners in private practice there is no legal requirement to undergo a DBS check as employers or the agency recruiting volunteers carry the responsibility for arranging for checks to be carried out on prospective employees. However, some practitioners may feel it is desirable for them to hold a disclosure and advertise themselves as having been checked, for the peace of mind of clients and their families. Although individual practitioners may not apply for an enhanced DBS disclosure on themselves they can either apply for a basic disclosure via Disclosure Scotland (even if outside Scotland) or use an "umbrella" organisation to carry one out on their behalf. The latter may incur extra cost on top of the fee set by the government for the DBS enhanced disclosure. The DBS website provides a directory of umbrella organisations who can be used to obtain a DBS disclosure.

Insurance

Practitioners who are planning to see children as part of their practice should ensure that their current professional indemnity insurance covers them for work in this field.

Summary

- It is important that practitioners give consideration to the setting in which they practice before beginning work with children and young people.
- The provision of some art and play materials can help younger clients feel more "at home" in therapy.
- A waiting area is an important part of the physical set-up for work with children and young people, particularly for allowing parents to stay on the premises while their children are being seen. Therapists must be clear about the boundaries regarding interactions with parents and others in the waiting area.
- Practitioners need to consider any administrative changes they may need to make when extending their practice to include children including considering obtaining a DBS check.

CHAPTER FOUR

Working with parents and families

Involving the parents and families of younger clients in the therapeutic work can present a challenge for practitioners. A general look at the literature on the subject reveals an array of differing views and opinions, indicating perhaps some controversy. Anna Freud (1965) conveys a sense of this in the following;

> The child analysts' techniques of dealing with the parents vary widely from the extreme at one end of excluding them from the intimacy of the treatment altogether, to keeping them informed, permitting them to participate in sessions (with the very young), treating or analyzing them simultaneously but separately, to the opposite extreme of treating them for the child's disturbance in preference to analyzing the child himself. (A. Freud, 1965, p. 48)

Although Anna Freud is speaking specifically about the work of a child analyst here, the same dilemma of how to manage parents in the therapeutic setting is also faced by the therapist working with children and young people in private practice. The first "technique" mentioned in the quote, that of "excluding them from the intimacy of the treatment altogether", is not generally a possibility in private practice. As seen in the previous chapters, working with this age group in private practice means confronting the question of when and how to involve parents or carers in the work, rather than whether to. Schools counsellors are perhaps more likely to be working in a context which excludes parents from the therapy, although they have the educational context to contend with in the place of the actual parents. This can sometimes create difficulties for counsellors who have been seeing children and young people in a school or college setting in making the necessary adjustments to include parents in the work that the transition to practising in this different setting demands of them.

Introducing the element of the parents into the therapeutic work can be complicated and demanding of the therapist, however, it can provide great benefits in terms of the progress of therapy with children and young people. This is most certainly not a recommendation for the direct involvement of parents in all aspects of their child's therapy, but rather an acknowledgement of the undoubted importance of parents and families in their children's lives, while dependent, and therefore in their therapy. Marks Mishne (1983) makes the point that a "family perspective" is a requirement for any form of child therapy. She goes on to say that, "The child cannot be treated in isolation, independent of the reality of the parents, the home milieu, and the needs of the sibs" (Marks Mishne, 1983, p. 206).

Involving parents and families

The first chapter of this book examined the referral and assessment phases of therapy, and looked at the involvement of the parents at this stage. Following on from this, the chapter on contracting and the therapeutic frame considered the review process, which involves parents and carers in the progress of the therapy, and allows their thoughts and views to be taken into consideration. So, from the very beginning of the process, parents and carers are likely to have been involved in the therapy of their children to some extent, and the way in which this has been managed by therapist and family members will already have had an impact on the work undertaken, both within the sessions themselves and in life outside of them.

When therapy is being offered to children and young people who are still living with and dependent upon their parent(s), it must be taken into account that these clients spend far more of their time in their family environments than they do in the room with their therapist, and they will go on living there after their therapy sessions have come to an end. Therefore the client's home environment could possibly be an important factor in creating and sustaining the benefits of therapy.

As outlined in the quote from Anna Freud at the start of this chapter, there are a variety of ways that parents and families could be engaged in their child's therapy. The following will outline a few of them and examine the pros and cons of various methods of engaging parents and family in the therapeutic process.

Family session—parent(s) and client together

The session where client and parent(s) are seen together is one which must be carefully considered before being embarked upon. It represents the entry of a third party in the form of parent(s) into an already established therapeutic alliance between therapist and client. It is arguable that the therapist and parent(s) also have a previously established relationship, and they may be more or less familiar with each other depending on the contact they have had at the referral, assessment and review stages of their child's therapy so far. A third pre-existing pairing is that of child and parent(s), and this may be more or less functional at the time when a meeting is considered.

Meeting with client and parents together can be extremely useful in allowing the client to communicate thoughts and feelings they have been exploring and learning to articulate in therapy sessions, to their parents, within an environment in which they feel safe and which is facilitated by someone in whom they have established some degree of trust. If the therapist can also create an environment in which the parents too experience some sense of safety then it is possible that family dynamics, which may be a significant factor in a client's difficulties, can be examined and hopefully treated in a way which will prove beneficial for the client.

The following case example demonstrates how a therapist might come to this decision, with his client, to meet with them and their family together and how such work might take place.

Case example—Mary and John

Mary is a sixteen year old girl in her last year of high school who has been referred for counselling due to her parents' concerns regarding her low mood. Mary has been meeting on a once weekly basis with her counsellor, John, for five weeks. She has increasingly been speaking of difficulties in her relationship with both her parents, as well as about the impact this is having on her mood. Mary reports her parents as being unwilling to allow her any freedom to go out with friends and take part in activities or attend parties at the weekend. They are, she says, insistent that she must focus on her schoolwork this year, in preparation for exams in the summer. Mary says that she is feeling isolated from her friendship group as she has nothing to contribute when they are talking at school and online about what they have been up to at the weekend. Mary is deeply upset at the weekends and after school when she knows her friends are out enjoying themselves, and she spends time alone online looking at their photos and comments about their activities. Mary admits that seeing what her friends are doing does lower her mood even more but she also feels the need to be connected to them somehow, and she hates it when her parents take her mobile phone or laptop away from her, due to their concerns that these devices are affecting her negatively. She reports having tried to discuss this with her parents and negotiate around the restrictions, but they have been unwilling to hear her point of view.

During their sessions, John begins to wonder if there might be some utility in meeting with Mary's parents for a session to discuss the impact of their parenting style on Mary's mood. He considers that they are clearly concerned for their daughter as they have referred her to him in the first place, and are paying for her sessions in the hope that her mood will be improved. He is beginning to believe that it is going to be hard for Mary's mood to change significantly without some change in their parenting style. John thinks very carefully about this and discusses his thoughts in clinical supervision. His supervisor suggests the importance of considering both the internal and external factors that may be affecting Mary's mood before deciding to discuss with Mary how she would feel about bringing her parents into a session. John says that he is fairly certain from what she has told him in their sessions that Mary's mood lowered when she reached a stage of adolescence where separation from her family and the forming of new attachments to her peers was appropriate. At this point her parents became far more rigid and authoritarian than she had previously experienced them, and her mood began to lower at this point as she became increasingly isolated from her peer group.

At their next session, John raises with Mary the idea of involving her parents in her therapy in some way. He believes that their therapeutic alliance is well enough established by this stage that Mary will trust that he will manage the boundaries in a way that both protects her confidentiality and keeps her best interests central. Mary is positive about this idea, and they discuss various options. At first Mary is keen for John to meet with her parents alone as she feels they will be more open with him if she is not there. John invites Mary to think more about how she will feel if her parents have had contact with John without her there and she decides that she would prefer it if they met together. They agree to suggest to Mary's parents that the joint session will be an "extra" and that Mary will have her weekly individual session as usual. They also agree on certain issues which have been discussed in the counselling sessions but which Mary does not yet feel she would like shared with her parents. They end the session having agreed that Mary will ask them the following day to arrange a session.

This example shows the counsellor weighing up the influence of internal and external factors on his client's presenting issues, and making a decision based on this consideration, as well as on his understanding of Mary's parents and their general concern for their daughter and wish for her mood to improve. John's decision here takes into account what he already knows of her parents through experience. If he were less confident of their willingness to be open to being involved directly in their daughter's therapy he might have reconsidered the idea. In this case, after discussion in supervision, John decides that external factors are a significant factor in the aetiology of Mary's depression and that her parents have the capacity to work with what emerges in the session. He therefore considers that a session with her parents would, in all likelihood, be of benefit to his client.

When a session is arranged with parents it is important for the therapist to reflect again on how this might be experienced by the parents as well as how the client will feel having seen their therapist in a different interaction than they are used to in their individual sessions. As mentioned previously regarding review sessions, parents may feel anxious about becoming directly involved in their child's therapy. They may experience it as exposing and fear that they will be blamed or undermined by the therapist in front of their child. As Glenn, Sabot, and Bernstein (1992) write of parents' fears regarding their children's therapy "They may anticipate a deadly serious dissection of their destructive role in the etiology of their child's illness" (Glenn, Sabot & Bernstein, 1992, p. 394). As with the review session in a previous chapter, it can be helpful to hold this in mind when meeting with parents in order to keep the session as reflective and constructive as possible.

The following case material returns to Mary and John and explores how the session with Mary's parents unfolds.

Case example—Mary, Frances, and Ian

Mary's parents, Frances and Ian, agree to come in for a session during the following week. In her final individual session beforehand, John asks Mary what her hopes are of the family session. She tells him that she would like her parents to understand better how their actions are affecting her. She believes that they will be more willing to listen to John than they are to her when at home. John asks her to consider how she might feel if the session does not go well and her parents are not able to reflect on their parenting behaviour in the way Mary hopes they will. Mary responds by saying that in that case she and John will have to continue to look at ways she might be able to improve her mood without things directly changing at home.

During the family session, which takes place later that week, Mary is able to raise with her parents her thoughts and feelings regarding the impact their parenting style is having on her mood. At first John observes Mary's mother reacting with anger to what she is hearing and trying to defend her position as a concerned parent who is protecting her child, rather than being able to engage with what Mary is saying. He tries to intervene appropriately in a way which might encourage all parties to hear each other's points of view.

Mary's dad seems more able to both hear and consider what his daughter is saying, and he points out to his wife where she is missing the point being made. Having become quite upset and tearful at this point, Mary's mum is then able to open up with her daughter and share the story of a traumatic incident which occurred during a party she attended when she was about the same age as Mary is now. This was not something which she had previously shared with her daughter as she felt it might frighten her, although her husband was aware of the incident. Frances is able to acknowledge that her anxiety about something similar happening to Mary has meant that she has felt the need to overly restrict Mary's opportunities for social contact. In Frances' mind, she was simply restricting opportunities for traumatic events to occur. Ian is also able to acknowledge that his concern for his wife meant that he had colluded with her need to overly protect Mary, even when he felt it was not the right way to be treating their daughter.

Both parents acknowledge that they have been aware all the time that this issue was quite probably affecting the way they were parenting and may have been contributing to Mary's problems, but they had felt unable to acknowledge this to themselves or each other for fear of unearthing something long buried. Although visibly upset, they both expressed relief that this was now being addressed.

As their time came to an end in the session, John asked the family how they had found it. He suggested to Frances that if she is interested, he can suggest the names of some therapists who might be able to help her explore and understand her early experiences further. He also suggests that they might meet again as a group in the future if this is felt to be appropriate for Mary's counselling.

This example shows how the intensive setting of a one-off family session can be used effectively to "unlock" anxieties and previous traumas which, if left unexamined, can have a powerful and deeply negative affect on a whole families functioning, as well as on an individual family member's ability to develop appropriately.

One of the skills demonstrated by the therapist in this extract is that of managing to allow the points of view and feelings of all present in the room to be heard and respected as appropriate, whilst keeping Mary and her therapeutic needs central in the process. The therapist's task in this situation is a complicated one. The therapist must establish a working alliance with the parents sufficient for them to feel safe enough to open up and engage fully with the therapeutic process, whilst not losing sight of the needs of the client. As Marks Mishne

(1986) notes; "... the objective in work with parents is to develop their insight into the connections between their problems and those of their child, to thereby enlist their efforts and involvement to help meet the child's evolving developmental needs" (Marks Mishne, 1986, p. 314). This statement makes it clear that parents are involved in the therapy in order to help their child. Should they wish to be helped themselves, which may be entirely appropriate, it is important for them to find their own space in which to do so.

Some children and adolescents are far less willing than the client in this example to entertain the idea of having their parents involved in their therapy, beyond their paying for it and, if necessary, transporting them to and from their sessions. If Mary had been unwilling to bring her parents into the therapy at this stage it would be important for John to work through this with her, helping her to understand her thoughts and feelings. Some children and young people are happier to try to communicate with their parents themselves outside of their sessions, possibly using the insights they have gained from their therapy. This may be for a number of reasons, but commonly is because the client has just begun to become used to the idea that the therapy session is their own private space, and they are unwilling to allow anyone else to intrude upon this. Some clients can be helped to write letters to their parents and other family members, describing their feelings and the affect that the family member is having on them. It is important for practitioners not to become fixed on the idea that the session involving family members is vital if the therapy is to move forward.

Family session—parent(s) without client

A session including the client and parents or family member is not always desirable. In the following case material we look at how a therapist might decide on a session with the parents only and at how that might benefit the therapeutic work with the client.

Case example—Daniel

Daniel is twelve and the middle child of three siblings all close in age. He has an older sister of fourteen and his younger sister is ten. He has been referred for therapy because of his parents' concern regarding his increasingly controlled eating and exercise regimes.

Daniel has been meeting with his therapist, Laura, for six weeks and she is becoming concerned that the therapy is not progressing. Although she and Daniel have been able to talk about some of his thoughts and feelings around eating and his body, there is no sense of him being able to change his behaviours and develop an easier relationship with food.

When she asks him about his family, Daniel reports that he feels that his parents and in particular his dad don't really like him. He says that he gets blamed for anything that goes wrong at home and that he is the target for his father's anger, rather than either of his sisters. Daniel begins to open up about how angry he feels towards his sisters, who he is also very fond of, as well as his parents, and he finds that controlling his eating along with over exercising is how he has developed a way to punish himself for these "bad" thoughts and feelings.

Laura begins to wonder if the work with Daniel's complex relationship with food and his body might be helped if his parents had some insight into how Daniel sees his problems. They think together about what he would want to say to his parents and how he would wish them to respond. Laura suggests that it might be possible for her to share some of this with his parents at their review session and asks how Daniel would feel about that. He agrees that this would be a great idea and writes a list of things that he would like Laura to share with his parents at the meeting. Laura asks if there is anything that Daniel would rather she did not share with his parents and they agree on the areas she is allowed to cover and those she is not.

When a therapist plans to meet with the client's parent(s) without them present, it is important that they are clear in their mind about what their role is in this context. Unlike in the previous example where there were several different pairings and relationships in the room, here the client is not physically present, but is held in mind by both parties in the session. The benefits of this might be that the parents feel able to be more open with the therapist about their personal lives, such as historical family events, relationship difficulties they may be experiencing, or their own physical or typo health. This kind of information can be extremely important in terms of helping the practitioner to understand more of the environmental background of the client. This can also be an opportunity for the practitioner to help the parent(s) or carers understand how their behaviour, or the atmosphere at home, may be having an impact on the client which is contributing to their presenting issues.

A disadvantage to meeting without the client present is the effect it could potentially have on the therapeutic alliance. Children and young people are generally not used to having their confidentiality protected by adults. They are probably more used to hearing their lives and difficulties discussed and fretted over by their parents with their friends, or other family members, and they may expect this to be the case when a therapist meets with their parents. As Ross (1964) notes;

> Most children, and particularly those being treated for emotional disturbances, have had important experiences which they entrusted to or shared with one adult, who promptly revealed the information to another, to the embarrassment and chagrin of the child. A neighbour, observing the child in some "forbidden" activity and rushing to tell his mother; mother telling father of the child's misdeeds; or parents sharing a laugh over something "funny" the child said or did are frequent childhood experiences. (Ross, 1964, p. 81)

It may be difficult for children and young people to imagine that their therapist will remain "on their side" in the presence of fellow adults. This difficulty can be lessened considerably by preparing for the meeting with the parents, in the session with the client beforehand, emphasising that their confidentiality will be maintained throughout the session with their parents, and that only information and content agreed upon beforehand will be shared.

In the following case material we see more of the family work with Daniel's parents.

Case example—Daniel

Laura meets with Daniel's parents in between Daniel's regular weekly sessions. His parents readily agree to the meeting, and arrive on time for their session. Daniel has prepared a sheet in his own individual therapy session that week on which he has outlined various occurrences which he feels exemplify unfair treatment by his parents. Before showing them the sheet, Laura asks Daniel's parents to tell her how they think the therapy is going, and whether they have noticed any changes in Daniel's behaviour at home.

Daniel's mum is tearful from the start of the session. She says that she is worried about Daniel's eating and says that he seems to be eating less and less, and spending more time exercising. Dad says that he feels that Daniel's behaviour is largely "attention seeking", and that he sees him as jealous of the amount of time mum spends with his older sister. Daniel's older sister is a talented gymnast who has to attend her club every day after school and often needs mum to go with her to competitions at the weekend. Daniel's younger sister is happy to go along with mum and sister to the club, but Daniel prefers to go running on his own. At the weekend dad says that he often spends time with his youngest daughter, but that Daniel generally doesn't want to be with them.

Laura notices that she feels quite protective of Daniel when his dad is talking about him and his "attention seeking". She is beginning to understand where Daniel gets the impression that his dad doesn't like him. She wonders what dad's thoughts are about boys and what their needs should be of their mothers, and whether Daniel's dad is somewhat dismissive or even envious of his son's emotional needs.

Laura decides to talk them both through the work that Daniel has prepared. She explains that there were things that had come up in their sessions that Daniel felt it might be useful to share with his parents. Laura tells mum and dad that Daniel feels jealous of the attention his sisters receive, and angry at what he sees as his "lower status" within the sibling group. He has given details on the sheet of some specific and recent incidents which he feels demonstrate this, and they look at them together.

After looking at the list, Daniel's dad agrees that he is harder on Daniel than on his sisters. He admits that he does let his anger out on him more than on the other two. He says that he is at work for long hours during the week and finds the stresses of home life difficult to deal with when he comes back in the evening. He finds the girls to be quiet and compliant, and therefore he responds more positively to them. Daniel's mum also mentions that dad seems to get on particularly well with their youngest daughter and that she is the most similar to him in character and disposition. Laura responds to this by asking them who Daniel most resembles or is similar to in the family. Mum replies immediately that she thinks Daniel is most like dad's younger brother, James, who dad believes has always been over-indulged by his mother. Daniel's dad says he is surprised to find that himself agreeing with this comparison, although he has never considered this before. He can see that his anger toward James may be interfering in his feelings for, and relationship with, his own son. He is not sure what to do about this, and seems quite anxious about what he has discovered.

Laura suggests to them that, while this may not be a complete understanding of Daniel's issues, it is a beginning to perhaps understanding some of the contributing factors. She suggests that both parents observe themselves and each other's responses to Daniel over the next few weeks, and see whether they are able to support each other in perhaps doing things slightly differently. She suggests that they consider having a further "review" session, either with just the three of them or with Daniel as well, in about a month's time.

This case material shows the therapist managing to help the parents find their own understanding of what might be contributing to their son's issues. Arguably, it might have been difficult for Daniel's dad to be as open to considering his own transference issues in this case, had his son been present. When a client's parents are seen without their child actually present they are relieved of the responsibility of being in the role of parent in the room. This relief meant that the parents were able to talk freely here about their different feelings for their children in a way that would have been much more difficult had Daniel been present. This can also be the case when parents talk about their feelings around the conception or birth of their children, problems bonding, or their general negative feelings towards a particular child. These are issues that a therapist will encourage a parent to talk about in this kind of space, and then help parents to understand how this might connect to difficulties their child is experiencing, and how they might be helped to make changes.

By way of parallel process, a therapist could also find themselves struggling with their own transferential feeling towards their client's parents, as in the following; "He may find himself blaming the child's parents, or in an attempt not to condemn them, the analyst may not notice their role in the pathogenesis of the child's illness" (Glenn, 1992, p. 399).

When issues such as these are encountered, clinical supervision is vital in order to help the therapist untangle their feelings regarding their client's parents or the client themselves so that the working alliance might be maintained appropriately.

A meeting with parents without the client present could be viewed as a kind of "parent guidance" (Marks Mishne, 1983) with the specific remit of supporting the therapeutic work being undertaken. It is not intended as a parenting intervention of the type that a social worker or family support worker might make. The intention of this intervention should be to look in depth at the client's relationships in their home environment, having already established in the individual work that there may be factors operating within the family which are contributing to the maintenance of the client's presenting difficulties. This is a therapy intervention which potentially; "helps the parents to help the child" (Marks Mishne, 1983, p. 250).

Working with separated, divorced, or reconstituted families

As noted at the start of this chapter, there may be added complications when working with children and young people where parents are separated and/or families have become "blended". In some families, life after a separation is established on positive lines and poses little or no difficulties in terms of the therapy, particularly when separated parents have established a co-parenting relationship which has survived the breakdown of other aspects of their marriage or partnership. In other cases, a child may be referred during the relationship separation process because of the emergence of difficulties related to the break-up of their parents' relationship.

Some practitioners may experience anxiety when asked to work with a child by a parent going through a divorce where there are disputes over child custody. There can be a concern that the parent's agenda for the therapy may be to use it to discredit the other parent and to prove that they are somehow not safe to have custody of their child. We will look more closely at the legal and ethical issues around this in the next chapter.

There has been substantial research into the emotional and psychological effects of separation, divorce, and remarriage on the children involved. As with all major life events, the effects on an individual child will be determined by a number of variables. These may include the child's age, their family circumstances before the separation and their relationship with each parent following the divorce, amongst others.

In their book *Surviving the Breakup: How Children and Parents Cope With Divorce*, Wallerstein and Kelly (1980), published the results of their five-year study of sixty divorcing families in California from 1971–1977. Their study looked at the impact of separation and divorce on the emotional, psychological, and social wellbeing of these families, and, in particular, at the 131 children of varying ages in the families in question. In their introduction, they describe divorce in these terms;

> Divorce is a process which begins with the escalating distress of the marriage, often peaks at the separation and legal filing, and then ushers in several years of transition and disequilibrium before the adults are able to gain, or to regain, a sense of continuity and confidence in their new roles and relationships. (Wallerstein & Kelly, 1980, p. 4)

When they began their study, their intention was to follow the families involved for one year, imagining that the issues would largely be resolved by that point, and their study complete. What they discovered was that the impact of divorce can be felt and observed for far longer than just one year, and the study was continued for five years with subsequent follow-ups. As they convey in the statement above, separation and divorce is a long and complex process, with a range of phases and an enduring impact on the lives of those involved. Practitioners in private practice are likely to receive referrals from families at various stages within this process. As with all issues encountered in practice, there is no single way in which children and young people will be affected by their parents' separation, divorce or remarriage. Practitioners will be required to utilise their skills in this context to listen to the client's narrative and help them to understand and make sense of the events they may be experiencing or have experienced in the past. The following section of this chapter considers in particular the impact of separation and divorce on therapeutic work which includes family members, exploring the particular factors which may need to be considered and attended to when working with a family which has experienced separation and divorce.

Separation

When a client is referred whose parents are in the process of separating, it is important to take this factor into account throughout the process from referral onwards. The initial referral may come from one parent or from both, although in cases where one parent is the main custodian they will often be the one making the referral. When taking the referral from one parent, the practitioner must consider if it is necessary for the other parent to be consulted or involved at that point in the therapy. Sometimes this will be done by the referring parent themselves. If the separated parents have managed to develop a relationship which allows them to focus on the needs of their children together, then the referral is likely to have been a joint decision, based on mutual concern for the wellbeing of their child. In these cases, therapy can proceed as it would with any other client, and either or both parents can be involved and included to the appropriate level, as they would in the therapy of a child with two resident parents. The practitioner in this case will be able to consider the breakdown of the parents' relationship as important background information for the therapeutic work, but not necessarily need to contend with its impact within the therapy framework and contract.

Where there is a less coherent and established co-parenting relationship in place, the issues may be more complex. When a child is referred in these cases there may be a desire on the part of one parent to exclude the other parent entirely from their child's therapy, or to present their child's issues as being exclusively the fault of the other parent. There may be a strong push for therapists to collude with this exclusion and agenda. It is important, if this is suspected to be the case, to try to encourage the referring parent to allow the other parent to be involved in the therapy to some extent. This is most relevant to work with younger children, where there is likely to be more parental involvement in the therapeutic process, but it can certainly also apply to work with adolescents and young people. Isaacs, Montalvo, and Abelsohn (1986) refer to this in their book *The Difficult Divorce: Therapy for Children and Families*;

> One aspect of therapy with families undergoing separation and divorce that is often overlooked is the obvious need for both parents to participate. In most cases one parent—usually the custodial parent—is concerned about the children and calls a therapist.

The other parent may be considered irrelevant in the treatment or
may be unwanted. (Isaacs, Montalvo & Abelsohn, 1986, p. 5)

The authors go on to stress the importance of both parents being
involved to some degree in their child's therapy, and that the child be
made their priority. Their contention that children are vulnerable to
separation within the family, and that bringing this to the attention of
both "warring" partners in the hope that they can use this to recognise
their impact on their children is illustrated in the following;

> Thus our primary treatment goal is for both parents to continue to
> be responsible for their children, despite the upheaval in their own
> lives. Toward this end, we help the couple develop their relation-
> ship as *parents*, as opposed to their relationship as *spouses*. It is not
> easy for people to preserve their parenting relationship while dis-
> solving their relationship as husband and wife. Those who succeed
> demonstrate a workable capacity to control their disagreement.
> (Isaacs, Montalvo & Abelsohn, 1986, p. 6)

Of course there are some instances where it may not be preferable or
appropriate to encourage the involvement of both parents. In situations where there has been domestic abuse or other abusive behaviour
towards the children or either partner, it may be important to protect
the therapeutic space from the prospect of further abuse occurring, or
of children or partners being re traumatised by the experience. In these
cases, the therapist must hold a delicate balance between identifying
that abuse has taken place and therefore imposing protective measures,
whilst not detracting from the client's process of exploring their own
feelings about their experience, within therapy. This is illustrated in the
following case vignette.

Case material: Mark and Leanne

Mark is six years old and has been referred for therapy by his
mother Leanne. When they meet for the assessment appointment,
Leanne mentions to the therapist that Mark witnessed some incidents of domestic violence between her and his father during
the end of their relationship. Mark has been referred for therapy
because of Leanne's concern that this may have had an impact on

him. At the moment he does not have unsupervised contact with his father, and Leanne feels that the contact he does have with his father is upsetting him. She says that his nightmares are more distressing following contact visits, and that his sleeping and eating tend to be problematic at these times. Leanne asks that Mark's dad not be informed regarding the therapy, nor be involved in any way in the therapy process.

   As at this point in time, the therapist is aware of a solicitor's letter indicating that Mark is not allowed to have unsupervised contact with his father, demonstrating to the therapist that there are some genuine concerns here for his wellbeing, and she decides to comply with the wishes of the parent in this case.

Here the practitioner can weigh up information regarding any actual legal issues around contact for this child in considering whether and how to involve the parents. This should enable the therapy sessions to be protected and made available for Mark to explore and express his own feelings and thoughts about what is happening in his world, within the therapeutic relationship.

This may be more difficult if a parent asks for the therapist to provide a report regarding the child's therapy sessions that they may wish to use during legal proceedings. Parents sometimes hope that their child's therapy will demonstrate and exemplify their own doubts around their ex-partner's capacity to parent. It is important for the therapist to remain committed to following the guidelines for ethical practice laid down by their professional body when a request such as this is made, as well as discussing it thoroughly in clinical supervision. As with other areas covered in this chapter, the therapist must keep in mind the rights of the child and their best interests at all times. In private practice there is the added factor, as previously mentioned, that the parent is generally paying for the therapy themselves. This might mean that if a therapist is not prepared to follow the parent's agenda in terms of producing a report for court which supports their aims in terms of custody arrangements, they may threaten to terminate their child's therapy. In some cases it may be that termination is unavoidable given the circumstances. This is an unfortunate and hopefully rare eventuality, but ultimately necessary if ethical boundaries are being challenged. If a functioning therapeutic alliance has been established at the beginning of the work, hopefully the therapist will be able to indicate to the parent how damaging for their child it could be for the therapy to be ended at this point. Some parents may be able to understand that this is of more importance than using the therapy as ammunition in a court battle, however this is by no means always the case given how high emotions can run at these times.

Case material: Mark and Leanne—Part Two

As the work with Mark continues, Leanne asks the therapist when they will have a "review" session as discussed when they first contracted. The therapist agrees that this should take place after six sessions, and an arrangement is made to meet mum alone outside of the session with Mark. Mark and his therapist discuss together what he would like to be shared with his mum and he chooses a painting he has done of the family dog and says he would like the therapist to show it to mum.

When the therapist and Leanne meet up, Leanne begins by asking her if she thinks that Mark is being traumatised by his contact with his father. The therapist asks Leanne what her thoughts are, and she replies that she is in the process of asking the family court to grant her sole custody of Mark with very little contact with his father, as she feels he is being harmed by their contact. She asks the therapist if she would write a report for Leanne's solicitor to support her case. The therapist replies that the therapy with Mark is confidential, and that, before providing any report, she would need to be certain that any breach of this confidentiality and disclosure of information was in Mark's best interest. The therapist goes on to say that Mark has only had six sessions so far and is just settling in to the work. He is beginning to explore and communicate in sessions and has been producing some art work, as well as using figures in the sand tray. The therapist shows Leanne the picture Mark produced and says that he asked for this one to be shared with her. Leanne tells the therapist that the dog was a family pet who had initially belonged to Mark's father before they got married. He had died six months ago, just when the difficulties between her and Mark's father began to escalate and erupt into violence. Mark was very upset at the time as he had grown up with the dog, and they were very close.

Leanne agrees with the therapist that Mark needs the therapy at the moment to be about coming to terms with what has happened between his parents. They agree that writing a report would not be beneficial at the moment. The therapist asks Leanne what support she has for her own trauma and to help her in dealing with what seems like a very hard process to be going through with Mark as well as the legal battle with her ex-partner. Leanne accepts the therapist's suggestion that she might find some therapy for herself, and they agree for a further review after Mark has had another six sessions.

Here the therapist has been able to diffuse the potential difficulty of the parent wanting a report for court at this stage by emphasising her original agenda for the therapy, that is, that of concern for her son's emotional and psychological wellbeing. The therapist in this extract remained calm and reflective when the request for a report was made, and was able to engage with the parent's genuine concern for her son, which could potentially have been eclipsed by her need for sole custody and to "win" her court battle. By demonstrating that the therapy was helping Mark, and that he was beginning to communicate his feelings and his experiences, the parent was able to let go of her need to make the therapy about something else. The therapist enhanced their working alliance by allowing the parent to see that she understood that this is an extremely challenging time for her, and by offering her an opportunity for support with this outside of her son's therapy. The therapist here demonstrates the usefulness of developing a working alliance with the parent which is then utilised to support and benefit the child's therapy.

When working with adolescents and young people in the context of considering work with other family members, divorce and separation can be important factors to take into account. In their research, Kelly and Wallerstein (1980) identified that those most vulnerable to the impact of divorce and separation were pre-latency children (under-fives) and adolescents. For adolescents already looking to challenge their parents' boundaries as they move toward their own separation and identity formation, family breakdown can be experienced as developmentally disturbing in many respects. Isaacs, Montalvo, and Abelsohn (1986) make the following comment on this;

In this situation of family fragmentation, common strategies employed by an adolescent are disengagement, distancing, and

attempts to connect elsewhere. The adolescent might be seeking
to escape from the toxic escalation of parental anger, depression,
and neediness or simply trying to find sustenance in the absence of
parental support and supervision. (Isaacs, Montalvo & Abelsohn,
1986, p. 184)

Where separated parents have begun to explore the possibility of a new
relationship or where new step-family relationships are forming, this
can also be disturbing for adolescents, who are themselves beginning
to work through issues around their own sexuality and desire to form
sexual relationships outside of the family. It is important that practitioners are aware of, and can consider, any background of separation or
divorce when thinking about the possible origins of a young person's
presenting issues. Adolescents can frequently experience intense loy-
alty conflicts, particularly if one parent has not remarried. The parent's
sexual intensity, which is likely to be reawakened with the new marriage, is also potentially anxiety-provoking for the adolescent with their
own emerging sexuality. For some young people, their own psychological and physical leave-taking preoccupations also lead them to such
intense ambivalence that their resistance to bonding with new step-
parents is considerable. For adolescents who may have spent some years
in a single-parent household, it is likely that they will not only lose status as the result of the remarriage, but they may also lose freedoms and
responsibilities which enhanced their self-esteem. These are important
factors to be considered when an adolescent is referred with issues such
as anger and acting-out by truanting, or disobeying parental rules, or
having problems adjusting to new family relationships. These complex
family dynamics need to be taken into account when involving others
in the therapeutic work. Parents can be unaware of the impact that their
new relationship or dating behaviour is having on the feelings of their
older and less dependent children, and it can potentially be very useful to bring this to their awareness, if their child's development is to be
supported.

Where there has been a remarriage for either or both parents, practitioners will need to engage with the challenge of working out who it
is best to involve in their child's therapy as well as whether and when.
Parents and step-parents can benefit from the kind of "parental guidance" discussed earlier in this chapter when they are struggling to
understand the impact of their relationship on the client's behaviour

and feelings. Here it may be useful to invite both parties into the therapy to think about this, if the client is in agreement. When issues around the parents' separation and the marriage break-up seem to be indicated in the presenting problem, it may be of more use to work with the separated parents together, if they are happy to do so and are able to put their own differences aside and focus on the needs of their child.

In therapeutic work with adolescents who may not want parents and step-parents involved in their therapy, it is just as important to have the family background in mind in order to help the young person gain an understanding of the context in which their difficulties have emerged. It may be helpful for them to think through their feelings of envy or embarrassment regarding their parents' dating practices, or their feelings of powerlessness if a new partner moves in. This thinking through can be done in the relative safety of the therapeutic alliance even if the young person does not feel comfortable discussing this with their parent.

In some respects, the subject of this chapter, working with parents and families, exemplifies one of the major differences in working therapeutically with young people rather than adults; that of whether we work with the internal world of the client or their actual environment. Anna Freud (1965) suggests that in the analysis of adults the work is primarily with the inner world of the client, their "psychic" reality. But she is clear that this is not the case in the analysis of children;

> For the analyst of children, on the other hand, all the indications point in the opposite direction, bearing witness to the powerful influence of the environment. In treatment, especially the very young reveal the extent to which they are dominated by the object world, i.e., how much of their behaviour and pathology is determined by environmental influences such as the parents' protective or rejecting, loving or indifferent, critical or admiring attitudes, as well as by the sexual harmony or disharmony in their married life. The child's symbolic play in the analytic session communicates not only his internal fantasies; simultaneously it is his manner of communicating current family events, such as nightly intercourse between the parents, their marital quarrels and upsets, their frustrating and anxiety-arousing actions, their abnormalities and pathological expressions. The child analyst who interprets

exclusively in terms of the inner world is in danger of missing out on his patient's reporting activity concerning his-at the time equally important-environmental circumstances. (A. Freud, 1965, pp. 50–51)

Working with parents and other family members can be complex and challenging for practitioners, particularly when their previous clinical experience has been in contexts which do not include such work. However, as Anna Freud states in the above, the home environment of the child represents an essential aspect of the therapeutic work, and failing to engage with this could interfere with a successful therapeutic outcome.

Summary

- Parents and families represent an important resource in therapeutic work with children and young people.
- Involving parents and family directly in the therapeutic process can support and sustain the benefits of therapy even after sessions have ended.
- There are various methods of involving parents and family in the work. These need careful consideration and consultation with the client before implementing.
- When working with children and young people whose parents have separated it is important to assess the possible impact of the separation on the child and, if appropriate, help the parents to understand this themselves.
- Children and young people are very sensitive to their family environments and therefore this is a vital factor in therapeutic work with this group.

PART II

ETHICAL ISSUES IN COUNSELLING CHILDREN AND YOUNG PEOPLE IN PRIVATE PRACTICE

CHAPTER FIVE

The law, ethical issues, and confidentiality

In all areas of work with children and young people, both in the UK and elsewhere, there are laws, statutes, and policies as well as ethical guidelines governing specific areas of that work. Many of these laws are enshrined in the policies of statutory agencies, and those practitioners who have worked in settings such as education or the health service are likely to have come across them in their daily working lives. When working in a school, for example, counsellors will need to have knowledge of the relevant safeguarding policy as well as know who the designated member of staff is for when concerns need to be reported. In turn, the school policy will have been originally drawn up, and continue to be amended, in response to government guidelines on the law relating to matters of safeguarding children in educational settings.

When working in private practice however, practitioners may feel less clear about what laws or guidelines are relevant to their practice as well as how the law might need to be applied to therapeutic work. It can follow that without the somewhat comforting clarity of a statutory or agency policy, therapists may feel a little "cut adrift" and "at sea" in this complex area of therapeutic practice. In the absence of such policy, private practitioners are more reliant upon their professional bodies as well as relevant ethical frameworks to assist them in their efforts to provide best practice in their work. However, they must also be aware of the relevant laws applying to their work, and confident enough to develop their own policies which are appropriate and relevant for working with this particular client group. The BACP states in the section of the *Ethical Framework* (2013) pertaining to "maintaining competent practice" that; "Practitioners should be aware of and understand any legal requirements concerning their work, consider these conscientiously and be legally and professionally accountable for their practice" (BACP, 2013, p. 10).

This chapter takes a careful look at the law and ethical guidelines as they apply to areas such as confidentiality, consent, and safeguarding children, as well as exploring how to combine a desire to work ethically and effectively with an adherence to important laws and government guidelines. It also shows how the private practitioner can draw up their own policies and guidelines for best practice. This exploration begins by looking at an area which is central to the role of therapist in any field; that of confidentiality.

Confidentiality

Ethical principle of confidentiality

In the "respecting privacy and confidentiality" section of the BACP ethical framework for counsellors and psychotherapists it states: "Respecting clients' privacy and confidentiality are fundamental requirements for keeping trust and respecting client autonomy" (BACP, 2013, p. 20). Counsellors and therapists are privileged with hearing intensely personal and private information from clients and their families. The therapist's role is to hear that information and consider its meaning with the patient, while holding it in confidence. This is how a therapist keeps the therapeutic space safe and builds trust with the client, therefore allowing therapeutic work to take place. The therapeutic relationship holds at its core the principle of confidentiality without which clients are unlikely to feel safe enough to share and explore the parts of themselves and their lives about which they have conflicted or difficult feelings.

Contracting for therapeutic work with both adults and children will generally begin with a discussion around the confidential nature of the counselling relationship and an explanation of the meaning of confidentiality in the context of therapy, along with an exploration of its limitations. With confidentiality at the core of the therapeutic relationship, clients are safe to share and explore all aspects of their story without fear that it will be exposed to others. The limits to this assurance are also defined in the contracting process, including explicit details of the circumstances under which a therapist would need or choose to break confidentiality and disclose personal information to outside agencies, with or without the client's permission. This is covered clearly by the UKCP (UK Council for Psychotherapy) (2009) ethical framework:

> The psychotherapist commits to respect, protect and preserve the confidentiality of their clients. The psychotherapist undertakes to notify their clients, when appropriate or on request that there are legal and ethical limits of that confidentiality and circumstances under which the psychotherapist might disclose confidential information to a third party. (UKCP, 2009, p. 4)

Legal duty of confidentiality

The principle of confidentiality in the therapeutic relationship is not only an ethical one, it is also upheld by the law. In *Confidentiality and Record Keeping in Counselling and Psychotherapy* (Bond & Mitchels, 2008), the law relating to confidentiality is explored in some depth. The authors outline some of the changes in respect of the legal duty of confidentiality brought about by the Human Rights Act 1998, and the Data Protection Act 1998, writing that; "One of the consequences of these developments, particularly the strengthening of the relationship between confidentiality and privacy, has been to simplify and widen the circumstances in which a legal obligation of confidentiality will arise" (Bond & Mitchels, 2008, p. 14) They go on to explain that regardless of whether a professional receives personal information directly from the client or person involved themselves or indirectly via a referral or even a mistake, there is still a duty to keep that information confidential if it can be reasonably assumed that the information was intended to remain private.

This concept has relevance in work with children and families where information is shared by a parent or carer during the referral, as well as when private information is shared by parent(s) at a review or family session, which might then be shared with the client. If this is to be the case, in the eyes of the law, it seems wise that the therapist informs the parents that they are likely to share some of the information they have been given with the client, or agree to a policy around confidentiality which parent(s) and therapist are happy with, and which remains in the best interest of the client.

Bond and Mitchel (2008) go on to say:

> The critical question in determining whether a duty of confidentiality has been created depends on the answer to whether there is a reasonable expectation of privacy. Lord Woolf examined how the right to privacy is now protected by the law of confidentiality following the Human Rights Act 1998 and brought these two elements together in a statement about how a duty of confidentiality arises.
>
> A duty of confidentiality will arise whenever the party subject to the duty is in a situation where he either knows or ought to know that the other person can reasonably expect his privacy to be protected. (See A v. B plc and C ("Flitcroft") [2002]) (Bond & Mitchels, 2008, p. 15)

It should be evident from Lord Woolf's statement quoted here by Bond and Mitchells (2008) that therapists have a clear duty to keep both information they receive from clients and from others in the course of their work confidential, and that they may be liable to action in the courts if they fail to do so.

Having established the importance of maintaining a duty of confidentiality in therapeutic work via an ethical framework and the law, we come next to explore the limits to this duty of confidentiality, which cannot be viewed as an absolute and inalienable right of all citizens.

In *Complaints and Grievances in Psychotherapy*, Palmer Barnes (1998) describes two differing views which might be held by practitioners; those of either "absolute" or "pragmatic" confidentiality. She writes; "The absolutist view, that no one but the practitioner should share the patient's confidence, can be very attractive in its simplicity and sureness. But it may well hamper best practice from a client's point of view" (Palmer Barnes, 1998, p. 41).

When an adult client contacts a therapist to make a referral, or attends their first counselling session, it may be that, initially at least, they and their counsellor are the only people in the world who are aware of their therapeutic relationship. At this point there could be said to be an absolutist confidentiality in effect. In reality this is only likely to be maintained until the counsellor comes to outline their policy on the limits of confidentiality, including supervision and record keeping, as well as the right to contact someone's GP should they believe the client is at significant risk of harm. Therefore, in general practice, the absolutist confidentiality seems to make way for a more pragmatic approach early on in the counselling relationship. If the client cannot agree to a limited confidentiality in these respects a therapist may decide that they are unable to begin therapeutic work with that person. Clearly this would be an issue to discuss in clinical supervision or with a professional body before making a decision.

As discovered in previous chapters, holding an absolutist view on confidentiality would most likely not be possible or even desirable in therapeutic work with children and young people, primarily due to the involvement of a third party, usually parent or carer, throughout the work. There are many potential conflicts with maintaining confidentiality in work with both adults and children, and it is important to understand, and possibly discuss them with clients, if the therapy carried out is to be both ethically and legally sound.

Limits to confidentiality

As established in the above, practitioners have a legal duty to keep their clients' material confidential in accordance with the law designed to protect members of the public from potential harm. However, the law is not absolute on this point. It protects the right of a person to confidentiality as long as to do so is of benefit to society, and in the public interest. This fundamental principle ensures that, where maintaining confidentiality is not in the public interest, the law will change course on this matter. The law protects clients in respect of their right to know, for the most part, if their confidence is to be broken, to whom and what the reasons for that might be.

Given these legal limits to the duty of confidentiality, when maintaining it is not in the best interest of the public, client or others, practitioners are faced with the dilemma of taking a different and potentially very difficult course of action in breaching a client's confidence.

The following is taken from the BACP *Ethical Framework* (2013);

> The professional management of confidentiality concerns the pro-
> tection of personally identifiable and sensitive information from
> unauthorised disclosure. Disclosure may be authorised by client
> consent or the law. Any disclosures of client confidences should be
> undertaken in ways that best protect the client's trust and respect
> client autonomy. (BACP, 2013, p. 20)

This guideline on ethical good practice encourages practitioners to continue to hold the benefit of the client in mind when considering disclosing client information and potentially breaking their confidence. In
ethical terms, the decision to breach confidentiality must be done on the
basis that to do so is in the best interest of the client. In legal terms it must
be in the best interest of the client or of the public in general to do so.

Children, young people, and the law on confidentiality

Much of the law examined so far has been relevant to most, if not all
counsellors and psychotherapists and their clients working in the UK,
and beyond. It is important to understand these laws as they relate to
all practice, but there are specific laws relevant to therapy with children
and young people, and specific ways in which the law is interpreted
when working with this group.

Something already mentioned frequently in this book is the concept
of consent, and as seen in the earlier chapter on assessment, this is a concept of particular relevance to work with children and young people.

The clause on therapeutic work with children and young people in
the BACP *Ethical Framework*, states;

> Working with children and young people requires careful con-
> sideration of issues concerning their capacity to give consent to
> receiving any service independently of someone with parental
> responsibilities and the management of confidences disclosed by
> clients. (BACP, 2013, p. 15)

The earlier chapter on assessment looked at how the law relating to
children was greatly affected by the Lords ruling on the Gillick case
(Gillick vs. West Norfolk & Wisbech Area Health Authority, 1985) and
the Children Act 1989. Both of these altered significantly the way in
which the rights of children are viewed by the law and, therefore,

by statutory and other agencies in the UK, particularly with regards to children aged below sixteen giving consent to receive medical and other treatments without parental knowledge and /or consent.

As noted earlier, the Gillick ruling made it clear that anyone offering treatment to a child or young person *must* consider them able to make their own choices regarding this treatment, if they have reached a point of sufficient intellectual and emotional capability to do so. The practitioner is required to make this judgement and must feel confident in doing so. In terms of confidentiality, this means that a child deemed to have reached "Gillick" competency can be considered to be old enough to have their wishes considered by law if a therapist decides to breach their confidentiality. The same right to confidentiality applies to them as to an adult, although there are differences in the circumstances in which a therapist might decide to break their confidence due to safeguarding legislation.

Children who have not yet reached "Gillick" competency cannot in legal terms consent to confidentiality in their therapy. In the case of children "of tender years" (Griffith, 2008), that is, those minors aged below sixteen who have not yet reached "Gillick" competency, the therapist must negotiate with parents, or those who hold parental responsibility, for the client in terms of how confidentiality will be managed within the therapy. This negotiation can allow the therapist to obtain parental permission for the content of their child's therapy to remain confidential on the basis that this is ethically important. It is important where there is no clear legal requirement for client confidentiality not to lose sight of its importance ethically.

"Gillick" competency or "sufficient understanding"

Table 5.1 below shows the UK government criteria regarding assessing for "sufficient understanding" in children aged under sixteen when deciding who is legally able to give consent regarding sharing of confidential information. This information is taken from the government guidance document, "What to do if you're worried a child is being abused" (HM Government, 2006). This guidance also states that:

> Children aged 12 or over may generally be expected to have sufficient understanding. Younger children may also have sufficient understanding. (HM Government, 2006, Appendix three, 4.17)

Table 5.1

4.18 The following criteria should be considered in assessing whether a particular child on a particular occasion has sufficient understanding to consent, or refuse to consent, to sharing of information about them.
 	
 • Can the child understand the question being asked of them?
 • Does the child have a reasonable understanding of:
     – what information might be shared?
     – the main reason or reasons for sharing information?
     – the implications of sharing that information, and not sharing it?
 • Can the child or young person:
     – appreciate and consider the alternative courses of action open to them?
     – weigh up one aspect of the situation against another?
     – express a clear personal view on the matter, or are they constantly changing their mind?

(HM Government, 2006).[1]

Worth noting in this guidance is the phrase "on a particular occasion". This confirms that "Gillick" competency and other judgements of "sufficient understanding" are context based and are changeable concepts. A child deemed as competent to decide to consent to confidential counselling at the age of twelve may not be considered as having sufficient understanding to consent to a high-risk medical treatment or procedure without parental knowledge or consent. It is also the case, as with adults, that although a child under sixteen may be recognised as of sufficient understanding and capacity to consent at one point of their therapy, this may not be the case at another point should their capacities change due to circumstances such as prolonged drug or alcohol abuse, psychotic breakdown or compromised cognitive functioning due to malnutrition as a part of anorexia nervosa.

Consent to break confidentiality

For all therapists faced with the need to not keep information disclosed confidential within the therapy, the first course of action taken should be to seek the consent of the client to break confidentiality, and for this to be agreed upon by both parties.

A previous chapter examined the "review" session where information about the counselling is shared between client, counsellor, and parents, and it was noted that any information gained from counselling sessions to be shared by the counsellor with other family members needs to be previously agreed to by the client. In such cases the therapist must have a conviction that it is in the client's interest for the information to be shared with the parents, and that this will benefit their therapy. Practitioners will be seeking to provide the best therapeutic service possible to their clients and, as already discussed, this can sometimes be best served by working in conjunction with other family members. If the client in this situation is unhappy for any information regarding their sessions to be shared then, as long as the counsellor believes that this will not put the client or another at risk, they must adhere to their wishes. In this case the duty to maintain the client's confidentiality is paramount.

When a practitioner does have concerns that their client may be at risk of significant harm, either from themselves or from another, they may consider that, ethically, it is in the client's best interest to break confidentiality. In such cases, it is important that the counsellor discusses their concerns with the client, and seeks consent for the breaking of confidentiality, unless to do so would be to increase the risk of harm either to the client, or to another child, or vulnerable adult.

Table 5.2 below shows the definition of "significant harm" as set out within The Children Act 1989.

Table 5.2
"Significant Harm"—definition as in The Children Act 1989
"harm" means ill-treatment or the impairment of health or development [including, for example, impairment suffered from seeing or hearing the ill-treatment of another]; 　"development" means physical, intellectual, emotional, social or behavioural development;
• "health" means physical or mental health; and • "ill-treatment" includes sexual abuse and forms of ill-treatment which are not physical.
(10) Where the question of whether harm suffered by a child is significant turns on the child's health or development, his health or development shall be compared with that which could reasonably be expected of a similar child. (Children Act 1989, 31: 9 and 10).

When a practitioner speaks of "significant harm" to a client, in legal terms they are stating that they believe there is evidence that the client's mental or physical health is threatened by behaviour by the client themselves, or by another, to such a degree that it could affect their healthy development and wellbeing. According to safeguarding guidelines, in these circumstances there is no longer an automatic duty to maintain the confidentiality of the child's disclosures. It will no longer be considered to be absolutely in the client's best interests to maintain confidentiality. The practitioner must then themselves decide, preferably in collaboration with their client, what the best course of action might be.

Safeguarding children

In contrast with the USA, where reporting of child abuse is mandatory by all professionals working with children including therapists (Child Welfare Information Gateway, 2014; Jenkins, 2007), there is no statutory requirement in England and Wales that therapists in private practice report suspected child abuse (Daniels & Jenkins, 2010). UK government guidelines on best practice for working with children make it clear that they are applicable to all professionals working with children, "whether they are employed or volunteers, and working in the public, private or voluntary sectors" ("Information sharing", HM Government, DfES, 2015). The more recent "Working Together to Safeguard Children" (HM Government, DfES, 2015) clarifies the roles and responsibilities of all professionals working in the UK with children and families in terms of safeguarding issues, although this guidance only applies to those in statutory, public, voluntary or community services, who are legally or voluntarily accountable to the ACPC (Area Child Protection Committee). It is, however, advisable for therapists in private practice to be aware of these statutory guidelines with regards to their own practice (Bond & Mitchels, 2008). The UKCP requires psychotherapists to: "… undertake to know and understand their legal responsibilities concerning the rights of children and vulnerable adults and to take appropriate action should the psychotherapist consider a child or vulnerable adult is at risk of harm." (UKCP, 2009, 1.9) According to Jenkins (2007), the ambiguity around the law on safeguarding for those outside the statutory remit renders the position of private practitioners; "… more complex. In effect they will have to exercise their professional judgement in deciding whether or not to report child abuse" (Jenkins, 2007, p. 160).

In *Therapy with Children: Children's Rights, Confidentiality and the Law*, Daniels and Jenkins (2010) argue the case that many children and young people choose to disclose sensitive information to a therapist precisely because of the confidentiality agreement as this allows them the space to consider what is happening, and to think about their position with another adult who can contain it for them while they do so, rather than telling a teacher or police officer who is likely to need to take immediate action on their behalf;

> It cannot be assumed that in these [case examples] and similar situations, the child client who makes risky disclosures within the therapeutic setting is simply asking for protection. If so, then it is wondered why they would elect to tell an adult who has made a pledge of confidentiality, rather than another adult who would readily act upon such information. It is possible that a child might not make a conscious decision to disclose such information at the onset of treatment, but that the therapeutic setting helps the child to discuss such issues, perhaps for the first time. (Daniels & Jenkins, 2010, p. 107)

Daniels and Jenkins (2010) argue that therapists often break confidentiality in child protection situations as a way of managing their own anxiety, rather than because they have their client's best interest in mind. The therapy contract which places limits on confidentiality as outlined in this chapter is also viewed by Daniels and Jenkins (2010) as coming more from the therapist's need to protect themselves rather than to protect the client;

> While this approach may reduce the therapist's anxiety, it may actually increase the anxiety of the child. In effect, the child's thoughts under this contract have been policed from the outset. The natural consequence under such a contract is for children to refrain from talking about what might be the most important issues in their lives … For some children such a contract is unclear and confusing; they may wonder exactly what information the therapist will contain and what will be disclosed. (Daniels & Jenkins, 2010, p. 109)

This argument is a convincing one: without absolute confidence that their disclosures will be contained how can a child or young person trust that their therapist will remain a container for their process, rather than someone who acts on their disclosures in their external world with potentially damaging consequences? This is certainly a question which therapists need to have in the forefront of their mind when contracting and working therapeutically with young people. There is a delicate balance to be struck here for the private practitioner between creating a therapeutic environment where children can express themselves without fear of exposure, and the need also to protect those children and others from potential harm. Therapists working with children in private practice need to be realistic about how much anxiety they can tolerate and, indeed, how much it is right for them to tolerate. Since the therapist in private practice is working without the somewhat "black and white" of mandatory reporting or being tied to agency or government guidelines they must continue to do what is necessary to enable them to practise in such a "grey area".

With this in mind, it is important that the counsellor in private practice is clear about what their own policy, compliant with current professional, ethical, and government procedures, for managing issues around abuse and safeguarding will be and how they will put it into practice.

Policies on safeguarding

So, how might a counsellor in private practice go about drawing up a policy on managing safeguarding issues in their work? In a later chapter we will look in more detail at the role of clinical supervision in the work of the private counsellor of children and young people, but it is important to mention it here with regards to any policy a practitioner might consider on safeguarding. For the private practitioner, often working in isolation with their clients, their clinical supervisor can play a vital role when it comes to issues around safeguarding. Their supervisor will usually be the first person that a therapist goes to when such an issue arises in order to consider their possible courses of action alongside a trusted colleague. As already established, confidentiality is a legal right and breaking it must be justifiable in the eyes of the law as well as ethically sound. Having a clinical supervisor with experience and knowledge of the law in this area can be invaluable for the private practitioner facing a dilemma regarding breaching confidentiality.

Other resources available for the practitioner are the government guidelines mentioned already. These are include; "What to do if you're worried a child is being abused" (DfES, 2006), "Working together to safeguard children: A guide to inter-agency working to safeguard and promote the welfare of children" (DfES, 2015), and "Information sharing—A practitioner's guide (DfES, 2015). It is also beneficial for practitioners in the UK to be familiar with The Sexual Offences Act (2003). These documents are all freely available via government websites (details available in the further reading section) and provide invaluable resources for the therapist wishing to work according to best practice guidelines in this area and also wanting to feel confident in their approach to this difficult area of the work.

It may also be helpful to let both clients, when appropriate, and their families know that, as a practitioner you choose to work within government policy on safeguarding the welfare of children.

Therapists may wish to use these resources to develop a series of questions to ask themselves either alone or alongside their clinical supervisor when it comes to considering breaching confidentiality. In the following case examples we will look at some of the questions a therapist might need to ask themselves when facing such a dilemma.

Safeguarding—Case example One

Bob is a nine-year-old boy who has been seen by a counsellor in private practice for about six sessions. Bob was initially referred for counselling by his mum who was concerned that he was waking during the night experiencing disturbing dreams and "night terrors". During his counselling sessions, Bob has spent a considerable amount of time using figures in the sand to show smaller animals being chased by large monster type figures. During his most recent session, Bob drew a picture of a family gathering where there was one monster figure amongst his human family. When the counsellor asked Bob to talk about the picture he disclosed that the monster represented his "uncle" (a family friend) who had apparently asked Bob to touch him sexually during the gathering which had taken place some months previously. The counsellor asked Bob if he would like to tell her some more about what happened, and Bob explained that the man had waited for him outside the bathroom and then took him back in there and locked the door. He then made Bob touch his penis, telling Bob that he was very special to him and that he mustn't tell anyone what had happened. He then unlocked the door and let Bob leave. Bob said that he felt bad afterwards, and was too scared to tell his parents as his dad is very good friends with this man and he thought his parents would be angry and punish him.

At the end of the session, the counsellor reminded Bob of the agreement they made at the start of their first counselling session that they would keep things between them as long as Bob wasn't in any danger from himself or anyone else. The counsellor explained that what Bob had told her today showed her that it seemed he certainly had been in some danger at the party, and that this was something his parents, and perhaps some other people, needed to be aware of. Bob said that he was afraid his parents, and especially his dad, would be angry with him, and that he wasn't sure he wanted the counsellor to speak to his parents at all. At this point he became quite anxious and was visibly shaking and beginning to cry.

This excerpt shows an example of a dilemma involving a non-"Gillick" competent child disclosing a possible episode of recent sexual abuse by a "family friend". The counsellor needs to consider why the child is telling them at this point, are they actually ready for the information to be shared, and what course of action is in the best interest of their client in line with ethical and legal guidelines. The client here has no legal right to confidentiality as he is under sixteen and would not be considered to have developed "sufficient understanding" to fully appreciate the implications and potential consequences of confidentiality in this case. The counsellor needs to consider the issue of whether "significant harm" has been done to the client, and also whether there is the possibility of significant harm being done again in the future to either this child, or another, as well as the possibility of a serious crime having been committed. In this case, as Bob is under thirteen at the time, the abuse, if proven, constitutes a serious crime under The Sexual Offences Act 2003. The therapist needs to consider this fact, as well as that the local authority, including police and social services, has a responsibility to protect the welfare of all children in their jurisdiction, and that they have the appropriate structures for the investigation of allegations of sexual abuse, which the therapist herself does not. As has been previously noted, however, there is no legal duty on therapists in private practice to report suspected child abuse to the authorities as Jenkins (2005) makes clear in the following extract:

> Hence therapists in England and Wales, who work in private practice, or for voluntary organisations outside the immediate ambit of the ACPC (Area Child Protection Committee) framework, are not bound by law to report abuse, although the ethical and moral pressures to do so may be considerable. Once again, the therapist could employ a public interest defence for breaking client confidentiality with some confidence in it being recognised as valid by the courts, in the unlikely event of ever being legally challenged by a client. (Jenkins, 2005a, p. 66)

Here is an example of a challenge for the private practitioner with no line manager or agency policy to be directed by in these circumstances. The counsellor could also be anxious about the impact that a disclosure may have on the therapeutic relationship, especially one which is relatively newly formed. However, they must also be aware that to not to break confidentiality in this case could be to put the client and possibly the public in general at significant risk.

Safeguarding—Case example One

The counsellor reiterates to Bob that when they met for their first session they agreed that they would keep things confidential *only* when Bob was not in any danger or at risk. She says that she believes that Bob has been in danger and could be again and that it is important that they discuss what he has told her with Bob's parents. The counsellor tells Bob that she will speak to his parents later that day and that she will only share with them what he has said about the man assaulting him in the bathroom at the party. She tells Bob that she will make sure his parents understand how difficult it has been for him to talk about this with her and how brave he has been in bringing it up. Bob seems a little happier but is clearly still anxious. He asks his counsellor what will happen now to the man and she says honestly that she does not know.

When the counsellor takes Bob down to his mum in the waiting room after the session, she lets her know that there is something she needs to discuss with her later that day. They agree to a time when mum will be free to talk on the phone, and arrange to speak then.

After this, the counsellor is careful to record all that happened during the session, and all that is discussed with Bob's parents after the session. The counsellor contacts her clinical supervisor by phone to discuss what has happened, and they agree to discuss it further when they meet for their regular supervision session later that week. The supervisor checks in with the counsellor regarding how she is feeling having heard Bob's potentially disturbing disclosure and the need to break confidentiality.

Bob's parents are clearly upset by what they have been told but they agree that the disclosure must be reported to the police and local social services. They are keen that Bob continue with his counselling.

In this case, although difficult for the counsellor to deal with, there was some clarity as far as whether or not confidentiality should be breached. The counsellor had made an agreement around confidentiality with Bob at the start of their work outlining the limits. This was also agreed with his parents at the time. In the situation described in the session, a serious crime had potentially been committed, and Bob had been in danger and could be again. Even if there is no specific legal requirement for therapists in private practice to report suspected abuse, there is a clear ethical responsibility here to protect the child from possible further harm. The counsellor cannot know what the relationship is between the family and this man, and whether he had regular access to Bob or to other children. It was important to break confidentiality and make sure the disclosure was reported to the relevant authorities for further investigation, which the parents, in this case, were prepared to do. Had they not been, the counsellor would have been within their rights to report it to the relevant authorities themselves. The counsellor might also choose to make contact themselves with social services anyway, in order for them to be aware of her involvement as a professional working with the child. Although in this example the counsellor chooses to tell the client's parents of the disclosure, there is no duty under law for her to do so if to do so may put the child or other children at risk, or if they are the potential abuser(s). Once a child protection case has been raised with social services they are legally responsible for communication with those with parental responsibility.

The government guidelines, "Working together to safeguard children" (DfES, 2015), shows clearly the procedure which will be followed by the local authority when an allegation of abuse of a child is made to them, via a series of flowchart diagrams. These provide useful information for practitioners in private practice, working outside of statutory organisations, without clear knowledge of what happens after the information is shared with social services and other agencies.

When the disclosure of abuse is made by a child over sixteen or who would be considered "Gillick" competent, the situation is potentially more complex. The counsellor must then seek the client's explicit permissions to disclose the abuse, which may not be granted. If consent to disclose is not given, the therapist then needs to decide if the client's wishes in this case outweigh the public interest. It is advisable for a counsellor in this position to seek advice from their supervisor, and other sources of professional legal advice before deciding to breach the client's confidentiality. A useful resource along with clinical supervision when a therapist is facing a dilemma regarding a potential breach of confidentiality is their insurance provider. Most professional bodies now require therapists in practice to have professional indemnity insurance and the insurance providers will be required to act on behalf of a therapist in the event of a complaint or court case. Therefore it can be very useful to discuss any potential breach of the legal duty of confidentiality with an insurance advisor before it takes place if possible. This is not necessary in the case of children under sixteen who are not "Gillick" competent where, as already established, there is no legal right to confidentiality. Many firms offer twenty-four hour legal advice helplines to assist practitioners facing dilemmas which may have potentially legal consequences. A further useful resource are counselling and psychotherapy professional bodies who can provide support and advice for therapists facing ethical and legal dilemmas in their practice.

In the next case example we examine a dilemma involving a child regarded as "Gillick" competent.

Safeguarding—Case example Two

Ellie is a fifteen-year-old client who has been seeing her counsellor for a year due to experiencing persistent anxiety attacks. On her return from her summer holiday, Ellie discloses that she was sexually assaulted by two seventeen-year-old boys, while staying at a holiday park. Ellie is very upset about what happened, particularly as she had been drinking with the boys before it happened, and had thought that they were her friends. Ellie tells her counsellor that she has told her best friend about what happened, but not her parents. She is adamant that she does not want her mum to know, or for anyone to report the boys to the authorities. When her counsellor asks Ellie why she doesn't want her parents to know what happened, she says that her mum always worries and overreacts and she doesn't think it would be helpful to tell her.

In this case the counsellor has a different set of considerations than in the previous example. Ellie would be considered by law to be Gillick competent and therefore entitled to her private information to be treated with confidentiality by law. She is of sufficient understanding to be able to consider with her counsellor the implications of maintaining or breaching confidentiality. If Ellie had had sex with either of the boys the counsellor may need to consider the Sexual Offences Act 2003. This act makes it clear that the age of consent for sex is sixteen, and therefore sexual activity with a child below this age is a criminal act. It is important to be aware that; "Sexual activity with a child under thirteen is an absolute offence, for which there is no defence in law" (Jenkins, 2007, p. 161). In this case Ellie has so far disclosed that she was sexually assaulted by the boys and that she did not actually have sex with either of them. Although her counsellor may consider that it would be beneficial to let her parents know at some point, or even for the incident to be investigated further and the boys held to account for their behaviour, the choice in this case remains Ellie's. She has the right to be able to discuss what has happened to her in her therapy, and for it to be kept confidential in the same way as an adult would.

Safeguarding—Case example Two

Ellie's counsellor explores in more detail with Ellie what happened with the boys on holiday. After the session the counsellor contacts her supervisor to discuss the possibility that this may be a safeguarding issue. Her supervisor confirms that she believes there is no need to automatically report what Ellie has disclosed in counselling to her parents. At her next supervision session the counsellor discusses the case further and they agree that this is not a safeguarding issue, and that confidentiality can be maintained in this case. Ellie and her counsellor continue to work to develop Ellie's self-esteem and ability to hold appropriate boundaries and keep herself safe.

If the counsellor in this case were to have breached Ellie's confidentiality, and spoken to Ellie's parents regarding her disclosure without consent, there is a possibility that the therapeutic relationship would have been significantly damaged.

In the following case example we look at a case where the issue is the client causing harm to themselves.

Safeguarding—Case example Three

Rose is a thirteen-year-old client who has been seen for several weeks by a counsellor in private practice. She was referred because of parental concerns that she was being badly bullied within her friendship group at school, and had started to binge eat and put on weight. During her weekly session, Rose discloses to her counsellor that she has been cutting herself when she is alone in her room in the evenings. Rose says she does this because it gives her some relief from the negative thoughts and feelings she experiences in the evenings when she is no longer busy with the events of the day, and that it is a way of distracting her from wanting to binge. Rose's counsellor asks if anyone else knows about the cutting, and Rose says she hasn't told anyone. The counsellor asks if Rose would show her and she lets the counsellor see cuts on the inside of her arms. The cuts are not deep but they do look red and sore and the counsellor is concerned they are not being looked after. Rose says she is worried that a family holiday is coming up and that her parents and siblings will see the cuts when she is wearing her swimsuit. The counsellor tells Rose that it is beneficial for her to have opened up regarding this behaviour and that now they will be able to work together at understanding why Rose does it as well as what it means to her. Hopefully they will work together to find ways of expressing and coping with feelings that do not cause Rose such pain and distress. The counsellor says that this may take time, but that this is what her counselling sessions are for. The counsellor says that she thinks it could be good to make Rose's mum aware of what is happening so that she can also be involved in helping Rose manage her feelings in a different way. Rose is frightened about this and says she doesn't want her mum to know. She expresses a fear that her mum will stop her from doing it and at the moment it is the only thing which makes her feel better apart from eating. She doesn't want to eat because her friends at school tease her for being a "pig" and being fat. The counsellor is concerned that if she goes against Rose's wishes and informs her mum about the cutting, Rose will no longer trust her enough to explore her behaviour in therapy, but she is also concerned that Rose may be at risk of significant harm if her parents are not made aware of what is happening.

This kind of example may be familiar to those working with this age group. Many young people harm themselves in a variety of ways, for a number of reasons. The work of the therapist in this situation is to help the client to understand what their particular reason for harming themselves is, in order to enable them to find alternative ways of expressing and managing feelings. Self-injury will be considered in more depth in the following chapter on working with risk, but for now it is important to consider what course of action her counsellor should take, from an ethical and legal perspective on the client's disclosure. Rose's counsellor needs to decide whether her client can be considered "Gillick" competent in this context, and therefore entitled to a legal duty of confidentiality, as well as whether she is at risk of "significant harm", according to the Children Act 1989.

Safeguarding—Case example Three

Rose's counsellor decides that there is no immediate life-threatening risk to Rose's wellbeing, and therefore she can maintain confidentiality at this point, and discuss the case in more depth with her clinical supervisor. They discuss Rose at their next supervision session and think carefully together about whether Rose can be considered Gillick competent. The supervisor asks Rose's counsellor if she believes that Rose has sufficient understanding of the consequences of keeping her self-harming behaviour confidential. They decide that she does and that she also has an understanding that she is not causing herself significant life-threatening harm by her behaviour at the moment. They decide that it is in Rose's best interest at this point for the counsellor to keep her disclosure of self-harming behaviour confidential, in line with Rose's wishes, but that this should depend on a further agreement between Rose and the counsellor that the self-harming behaviour be monitored at her counselling sessions. The counsellor makes it clear to Rose when they next meet that this is the basis on which confidentiality can be maintained and they agree that, should her self-harm become more serious, her parents will need to be involved. They will also consider how it might be possible to speak to her mum about the self-harm before the family holiday in a few weeks' time. Rose's counsellor suggests that it may be possible and appropriate to use a review session to do this when they can talk about it together in a supportive and containing environment.

This example demonstrates the importance of clinical supervision in providing space to consider different dimensions of a situation where concerns about safeguarding are raised. There is unlikely to be a definite right way for the therapist to proceed where a dilemma around confidentiality and/or "Gillick" competency has arisen, and therefore it is more important to ensure they have good enough information and support to enable them to consider their particular dilemma in the context of the relevant legal and ethical structures. If this is the case then the therapist, along with their clinical supervisor, should be able to arrive at a resolution which is both ethically and legally defendable and which both counsellor and supervisor feel is a good basis for continuing the therapeutic work in the client's best interest.

Breaching confidentiality without consent

There are some occasions in the therapeutic work when it is necessary to breach confidentiality without consent and even, very occasionally, without informing the client that this is going to happen. In the UK, the Terrorism Act 2000;

> makes it a failure to disclose, without reasonable excuse, any information which he either knows or believes might help prevent

another person carrying out an act of terrorism or might help in bringing a terrorist to justice in the UK. (Bond & Mitchels, 2008, p. 23)

This is an example of where the maintenance of a client's right to confidentiality would be seen to be in conflict with the wider public interest, and could therefore not be legally maintained. In the area of the prevention of serious crime, the courts are likely to accept that a therapist's breaching of confidentiality was done in good faith that it was in the public's best interest.

Data protection and record keeping

The final area of the application of the law to practice this chapter will explore is that of data protection and record keeping, specifically as it relates to children and young people. It has already been established in this chapter that young people over sixteen, or those under sixteen but considered "Gillick competent", have a legal and ethical right to confidentiality of their counselling sessions, and this extends to any records a therapist may keep about them according to the Data Protection Act 1998.

Therapists in general have very differing views and practices as far as keeping notes and record of sessions as concerned. There is indeed no legal requirement that therapists keep notes of their client work (Bond & Mitchell, 2008). The BACP advises therapists to "keep appropriate records of their work with clients unless there are good and sufficient reasons for not keeping any records" (BACP, 2013, p. 6) and the UKCP requires their members to "keep such records as are necessary to properly carry out the type of psychotherapy offered" (UKCP, 2009, 8.1). In spite of there being no legal requirement to keep client notes, most therapists choose to do so on the basis of wanting to provide good ethical and professional practice. Keeping notes enables them to reflect on their work with particular clients, as well as acting as an aide memoire, especially when practitioners are holding a large caseload. Records of clients' contact and GP details are also arguably essential for the practitioner working in private practice. The counsellor working for an agency or in an organisational setting will often be required to keep notes and records of clients in accordance with agency procedures. The counsellor in private practice must arrive at their own system for record keeping which is legally and ethically sound. The BACP guidelines in this respect are for practitioners to; "… take into account their responsibilities and their clients' rights under data protection legislation and any other legal requirements" (BACP, 2013, p. 5). Therapists working with children and young people may need to be particularly careful when keeping notes around disclosure of potential safeguarding issues as these may be required in the case of court proceedings.

The relevant UK law covering the keeping of records and personal information is the Data Protection Act 1998. This law is complex and it can be difficult for therapists to understand in which way it relates to their practice. The law says that if records are kept either manually or on computer in what the law would identify as a "relevant filing system" then they are covered by the Data Protection Act. A "relevant filing system" is "defined as 'any set of information' that is structured, either by reference to individuals or by reference to criteria relating to individuals in such a way that specific information relating to a particular individual is readily accessible" (Bond & Mitchel, 2008, p. 60). In accordance with data protection legislation, clients have a legal right of access to all information held about them in such "relevant filing systems". This extends to children aged sixteen or over or considered "Gillick" competent. It is important for practitioners to be aware of this and keep it in mind when making notes and deciding how to keep them. The law relating to a therapist's "process" notes (notes made after sessions where counsellors consider different aspects of the session) is less clear but it seems that if such notes are included in a client's file in the "relevant filing system" they would be considered to be covered by data protection legislation. If a therapist in private practice holds any information about their clients or records of sessions on a computer or other device such as smartphone or tablet then they must notify the Information Commissioner's Office and register for a small annual fee as a "data controller" and be included in the online register. A more detailed exploration of the law relating to record keeping and data protection is beyond the scope of this chapter. For a more comprehensive exploration of this important aspect of practice please see the further reading section.

Summary
– Achieving best practice in counselling children and young people requires a combination of legal and ethical considerations. – Therapeutic work with children and young people requires special consideration around issues of confidentiality and consent. – Practitioners in private practice will benefit from drawing up their own policies on confidentiality and safeguarding in accordance with current government guidelines for professionals in this field. – Practitioners need to consider data protection legislation regarding record keeping and confidentiality. Children aged sixteen and over and those deemed to be "Gillick" competent have the same rights as adults with regard to data protection legislation.

Note

1. This guidance updated March 2015. Please see reference section for more information.

CHAPTER SIX

Working therapeutically with risk

In therapeutic work with children and young people, issues of risk can present in many different forms. In this chapter we will look at specific areas of risk such as self-harm, eating disorders, sexual behaviours, drug and alcohol use, and mental health issues. The chapter is intended to offer support to the private therapy practitioner working outside of the regulation and relative containment of school, or agency guidelines.

What is "risk"?

Before going on to look at the specific areas where the question of "risk" arises, it is first important to consider what is meant by the term, particularly in the context of therapy. The Oxford English Dictionary defines risk in the following;

1. (Exposure to) the possibility of loss, injury, or other adverse or unwelcome circumstance; a chance or situation involving such a possibility. Freq. with *of*.

a. As a count noun. Freq. in *to run* (also *take) a* (also *the) risk* (also *risks),
    to run one's risk. cancer, occupational risk,* etc.: see the first element
    (OED online, 2014).

Risk in these terms can be a significant element in therapeutic work
with children and young people. Sometimes a child's "risky" behaviour is what determines the initial referral. For example, in the case of
a possible eating disorder, the parent might fear that the child's refusal
to properly take in nourishment is putting them at risk of malnutrition
or severe illness. Sometimes the genuinely risky behaviour has yet to
surface when the child first arrives in therapy, ostensibly for some other
reason. We may find that it is only as the therapeutic alliance forms, and
the client begins to trust the therapist and the therapeutic process, that
they can begin to share details of their risky behaviour, as in the case
example of "Rose" in the previous chapter, who could only talk about
her self-harm once the therapy had begun and she felt safe enough to
do so. Whether the risky behaviour constitutes the original reason for
the referral, or is revealed further into the work, the risk that is under
consideration may have an emotional or psychological basis which can
be engaged with via therapy.

Children, young people, and risk

As a background to thinking about risk, it is important to consider the
place of risk in human development and in children's lives. Children
and young people are natural risk takers and it is developmentally
appropriate that they should be so. This is an aspect of development
particularly identified by attachment theory (Bowlby, 1973), which
examines the relationship between separation and attachment inherent
in an infant's development.

When a healthy infant first crawls across the floor to examine an
interesting toy, they are taking a risk that it is safe for them to do so;
that the activity will be rewarding for them, and that they will be able
to return to the safety of their carer if necessary. The toddler who
subsequently makes their first wobbly attempt to stand up without
support is equally a risk taker. The outcome of their action cannot be
certain; they have not done it before, they have to take a risk, generally with the encouragement of parents and other onlookers. It is
also a natural part of the life of the older child and the adolescent to

take risks. Perhaps culturally there is an enhanced awareness of the risk-taking of adolescents because they are beginning to engage with the wider world in their explorations, and not just with toys or their home environment. To parents and other onlookers, this can seem more dangerous than when their risky behaviours are confined to the relative safety of the home or school environment, and might well prove so. Indeed, in adolescence; "overall morbidity and mortality rates increased 200% compared to childhood due to problems in self-agency, as evinced by the high ratio of reckless or aggressive behavior, substance abuse and suicide" (Stortelder & Ploegmakers-Burg, 2010, p. 507). However, risk-taking could also be viewed as a positive and necessary part of an adolescent's life too, their confidence in their abilities increasing as they take risks which allow them to "learn to understand and appreciate the consequences of their behaviour" (Poynton, 1997, p. 6).

The notable "risky behaviours" outlined earlier in this chapter are examples of when a child's exploratory behaviour seems likely to result in a negative, rather than positive, outcome, and runs the risk of causing them "significant harm" as defined previously. With adolescents, risky behaviour could be understood as an attempt at separation and autonomy as well as an anxious attempt to re-engage the parent and retain safety. An example of this is self-harm, which could be viewed as both the child's attempt to take some "ownership" or stake a claim to their body and life in the face of controlling or intrusive parents, at the same time as potentially raising parental anxiety if and when discovered. In writing about "character disorders" and the "antisocial tendency", Winnicott (1965) could equally have been writing about the kind of risk-taking behaviours being discussed in this chapter. For Winnicott, this tendency represents an attempt by the child or young person to return to a previous developmental phase; "The antisocial tendency always arises out of a deprivation and represents the child's claim to get back behind the deprivation to the state of affairs that obtained when all was well" (Winnicott, 1965, p. 204). This dynamic is particularly likely to emerge in adolescence, as it is at this point in life that children are attempting a psychological separation from their parents, as a precursor to the physical separation and independence of adulthood. As Winnicott suggests in the above, if this transition proves overwhelming for them for some reason, there may be an attempt by their psyche to return them to a point prior to the crisis.

Whatever theories are utilised in helping practitioners attempt to understand risky behaviour in their clients, the main focus of therapy must be to help the client understand their behaviour themselves. In my opinion, private practice has an advantage over other services for young people in this respect, in that it potentially offers the opportunity to work open-ended or longer term than school or agency services often can, thus allowing the client more space to develop understanding over time, without the pressure to have resolved the complex issues underlying the behaviour within a rigid timescale. Also, as discovered in the previous chapter, practitioners in private practice are not as strictly bound by safeguarding criteria or agency policies on issues such as drug and alcohol use or self-harm as other services are. This is not to say that these policies are unimportant or unnecessary; simply that without an official obligation to report or treat disclosures in a prescribed way, it may prove possible to offer a different kind of therapeutic space to children in private practice, allowing the development of an understanding of their behaviour which is unique to the individual client.

In order to provide this kind of space where the meaning of behaviour can be explored and understood, it is important that there are clear boundaries, supported by an understanding of how to work with risk behaviours when presented by the client. At the same time as providing a therapeutic space where risky behaviour can materialise and be understood, there must also be awareness and respect for the actual "real-life" risk-taking behaviour which is being exhibited. For example, it would not be ethical to simply examine in therapy the underlying reasons why a child is harming themselves without also recognising and addressing the dangerous, and potentially life-threatening, behaviour they are engaging in. This chapter and the following one on "referring on" will look in-depth at the realities of working with risk for the private practitioner, and illustrate how this can best be done ethically and safely for client and practitioner.

Significant risk of harm

The previous chapter looked in some depth at the concept of significant harm, as defined by The Children Act 1989, particularly as it relates to confidentiality, and this is useful to return to now. The therapeutic contract outlines both the importance of establishing confidentiality and of understanding its limits. This contract is intended to communicate to clients that session content will remain confidential until the material suggests the possibility of significant harm, from themselves or another. Practitioners are not in a position to be able to address behaviour which occurs outside the boundaries of the therapeutic relationship; therefore if they are concerned that the client is not going to be able to keep themselves safe from significant harm outside of the session then they must consider how best to respond to those concerns and possibly alert others, outside of the therapy, whom they believe, to the best of their knowledge, will be able to ensure the safety of the client.

As previously outlined, there are specific legal and ethical boundaries regarding confidentiality which provide a solid framework for the therapeutic relationship, enabling therapists to offer a safe space where difficult aspects of children and young people's lives and experiences can be encountered and understood. In this respect, an adolescent bringing details of their risk-taking behaviour into the consulting room may unconsciously be looking for "containment" (Bion, 1959) of difficult or hard to manage feelings. In this respect, risk-taking behaviour in adolescence could be viewed as a hopeful attempt to complete a developmental task which could not be facilitated by their environment in infancy. The words used by Bott Spillius (1992) to describe the task of the mother in managing the projective-identifications of her infant could also apply to the therapist in this context;

> If she is capable of understanding and accepting the feelings without her own balance being too disturbed, she can "contain" the feelings and behave in a way toward her infant that makes the difficult feelings more acceptable to him. He can then take them back into himself in a form that he can manage better. (Bott Spillius, 1992, p. 61)

With this in mind, it may be beneficial for the therapist working with children and young people to have had, or be in their own therapy as well as supported by good clinical supervision, so they are able to act with awareness if they are at risk of becoming overwhelmed by or over-involved in the client's material or projections. Marks Mishne (1986) comments on this in relation to work with adolescents;

> This [personal treatment] is necessary in order for the practitioner to develop a therapeutic, objective, emphatic response that

embodies the necessary self-awareness and self-observation, and
that controls against regression and acting out through, and/or
with, adolescent patients. (Marks Mishne, 1986, p. 5)

Very often children and young people who engage in risk-taking
behaviours such as eating disorders or self-injury have been carrying
unbearable loads of difficult feelings for some time with no sense of
there being anyone available to help to facilitate the containment and
integration of these feelings. Therefore, when they arrive in therapy and
are able to establish a safe enough working alliance with the therapist,
children may release large amounts of this feeling in the form of projections which the therapist must be prepared to manage and contain.
In order for the therapist to be available and open to this material they
will need themselves to have worked through their own difficulties suf-
ficiently to be able to help the young client with theirs. If this is not the
case there is a danger that the therapy may become stuck and unhelpful
in some way and that the client may terminate abruptly, often to the
relief of the therapist who may not have been aware of their own struggle with the client's material. In his original paper outlining the concept
of containment, "Attacks on Linking", Bion (1959) makes the point that
when the difficult feelings cannot find a home in the original "object"
it can actually intensify the original feelings and make them harder to
contain. With this in mind it is important to foster a therapeutic attitude
which allows clients to experience their difficult feelings as manageable
by another and that therapy will be able to help them towards their successful integration and management.

Identifying risk

The next section of this chapter will examine specific presenting issues
where risk behaviours can be a factor, and explore how best the practitioner in private practice can approach them.

Eating disorders

Issues around eating and body image can be common presentations
amongst children and young people attending therapy, often raising
some anxiety in the therapists working with them. For some children

attempting to manage the physiological changes of puberty, as well as to separate and become autonomous, food and diet can become an arena where these developmental struggles are enacted. What practitioners need to establish in therapy with children is when and whether issues expressed via food and the body constitute risk and/or significant risk of harm. It is important therefore, that therapists have some understanding of eating disorders and are able to act with awareness when behaviour around food and eating may be developing into a specific eating disorder, potentially requiring additional treatment if significant harm to the young person is to be prevented.

Diagnostic criteria

Both *The Diagnostic and Statistical Manual of Mental Disorders*, fifth edition (DSM-5) and The *ICD-10 Classification of Mental and Behavioural Disorders* (ICD-10), contain precise diagnostic criteria for a range of eating disorders. The criteria for both anorexia nervosa and bulimia nervosa are outlined in brief in the table below.

Table 6.1 below shows that the clinical diagnosis of an eating disorder consists, in simplest terms, of symptoms of a prevailing anxiety, generally that of becoming "fat", some behavioural adaptations in response to this fear; that is, restricting, purging etc., and a physiological or developmental impact such as severe weight loss and amenorrhoea (ceasing of menstrual cycle).

As there are physiological symptoms and concerns as well as psychological and emotional ones with eating disorders, some practitioners in private practice will need to work as part of a team where the physiological aspects are managed by other professionals. This will be looked at in more detail in a later chapter on working with other agencies, but for now it is important to note that this is a decision to be made on a case by case basis. Working as a team can mean anything from ensuring that the client's GP is also aware of the issue, to working alongside other professionals including, for example, a psychiatrist and dietician. It can be helpful for practitioners working with eating disorders to know that any necessary re-feeding and weight management are taken care of outside of the therapeutic space, leaving them free to concentrate on helping the client to understand, and hopefully resolve the underlying psychological and emotional issues.

Table 6.1. DSM and ICD Diagnostic criteria for anorexia and bulimia nervosa.

Anorexia nervosa	*Bulimia nervosa*
DSM-5: To be diagnosed with anorexia a person must display:	**DSM-5: To be diagnosed as having Bulimia Nervosa a person must display:**

• Persistent restriction of energy intake leading to significantly low body weight (in context of what is minimally expected for age, sex, developmental trajectory, and physical health).
• Either an intense fear of gaining weight or of becoming fat, or persistent behaviour that interferes with weight gain (even though significantly low weight).
• Disturbance in the way one's body weight or shape is experienced, undue influence of body shape and weight on self-evaluation, or persistent lack of recognition of the seriousness of the current low body weight.
• **Subtypes:**
Restricting type
Binge-eating/purging type.
	• Recurrent episodes of binge eating. An episode of binge eating is characterised by both of the following:
	  • Eating, in a discrete period of time (e.g. within any two-hour period), an amount of food that is definitely larger than most people would eat during a similar period of time and under similar circumstances.
	  • A sense of lack of control over eating during the episode (e.g. a feeling that one cannot stop eating or control what or how much one is eating).
	• Recurrent inappropriate compensatory behaviour in order to prevent weight gain, such as self-induced vomiting, misuse of laxatives, diuretics, or other medications, fasting, or excessive exercise.
	• The binge eating and inappropriate compensatory behaviours both occur, on average, at least once a week for three months.
	• Self-evaluation is unduly influenced by body shape and weight.
	• The disturbance does not occur exclusively during episodes of Anorexia nervosa.

(Continued)

Table 6.1. Continued.

ICD-10: to be diagnosed with anorexia nervosa a person must display the following:	ICD-10: to be diagnosed with bulimia nervosa a person must display the following:
• Body weight is maintained at least fifteen per cent below that expected (either lost or never achieved). • Prepubertal patients may show failure to make the expected weight gain during the period of growth. • The weight loss is self-induced by avoidance of "fattening foods". One or more of the following may also be present: self-induced vomiting; self-induced purging; excessive exercise; use of appetite suppressants and/or diuretics. • There is body-image distortion in the form of a specific psychopathology whereby a dread of fatness persists as an intrusive, overvalued idea and the patient imposes a low weight threshold on himself or herself. • A widespread endocrine disorder involving the hypothalamic—pituitary—gonadal axis is manifest in women as amenorrhoea and in men as a loss of sexual interest and potency. • If onset is prepubertal, the sequence of pubertal events is delayed or even arrested (growth ceases; in girls the breasts do not develop and there is a primary amenorrhoea; in boys the genitals remain juvenile).	• There is a persistent preoccupation with eating, and an irresistible craving for food; the patient succumbs to episodes of overeating in which large amounts of food are consumed in short periods of time. • The patient attempts to counteract the "fattening" effects of food by one or more of the following: self-induced vomiting; purgative abuse, alternating periods of starvation; use of drugs such as appetite suppressants, thyroid preparations or diuretics. When bulimia occurs in diabetic patients they may choose to neglect their insulin treatment. • The psychopathology consists of a morbid dread of fatness and the patient sets herself or himself a sharply defined weight threshold, well below the premorbid weight that constitutes the optimum or healthy weight in the opinion of the physician. There is often, but not always, a history of an earlier episode of anorexia nervosa, the interval between the two disorders ranging from a few months to several years. This earlier episode may have been fully expressed, or may have assumed a minor cryptic form with a moderate loss of weight and/or a transient phase of amenorrhoea.

Aetiology of eating disorders

There are a range of theories regarding the aetiology of eating disorders, ranging from biological and genetic models to environmental and interpersonal theories. It is beyond the scope of this chapter to go into them all in detail but further reading in this area is recommended.

However, one aspect of the aetiology of eating disorders which is relevant for consideration here is the question of why their onset is so often just prior to or during adolescence. Having some understanding of this can be very useful when considering treatment plans. In a chapter outlining "Developmental disturbances" and disorders of food intake in infancy, Anna Freud (1965) begins to demonstrate the links between infantile communications via food and those which emerge later in adolescent eating disorders;

> Battles about eating the mother's food express the toddler's ambivalent relationship to her. An excellent clinical illustration of this was a toddler who, when angry with his mother, not only spit out what she had fed him, but also scraped his tongue of any morsel of food adhering to it. Literally he "would have none of her". (A. Freud, 1965, p. 160)

Several theorists and clinicians writing about eating disorders suggest that the origins of the symptoms may be in the child's early experiences with their primary caregiver, particularly in the area of separation and individuation. For psychoanalyst, Hilde Bruch (1973), eating disorders are the result of the failure of the primary caregiver to react responsively to cues regarding their child's needs. The caregiver in this case is more preoccupied with her own feelings and on the infant's impact upon her. This kind of early experience of relationships provides little opportunity for the infant to gain a sense of their own identity and needs, but rather they become keenly attuned to the needs and wants of their caregiver. Bruch (1973) writes;

> A child growing up in this way may acquire the façade of adequate functioning by robot-like submission to the environmental demands. The gross defect in initiative and active self-experience will become manifest when he is confronted with new situations for which the distorted routines of his background have left him unprepared. (Bruch, 1973, p. 57)

This view is shared by clinical psychologist, Alan Carr (1999), who writes that;

> Children with eating disorders have difficulty learning how to interpret need-related internal physiological states and develop a coherent sense of self, because their mothers adopt a parenting style in which parental needs for control and compliance take primacy over the child's need for self-expression and autonomy. (Carr, 1999, p. 683)

While the psychiatrist and expert in the field of anorexia, Arthur Crisp (1983) writing in the *British Medical Journal*, considers that the roots of anorexia nervosa are often to be found in anxiety regarding separation, sexuality, and the adult body which are likely to be triggered during puberty although can, of course, come earlier or later as well; "To the anorectic the body, especially the adult body, is perceived as alien and threatening rather than owned" (Crisp, 1983, p. 856).

Anorexia nervosa can therefore be viewed as the psyche's attempt to hold on to, or return the body to the pre-puberty condition. While work begins on understanding these underlying issues, therapy may also be required to help the client to negotiate the emotional impact arising from resolving their symptoms and beginning recovery, which can entail gaining weight and, "re-entering" puberty; "As puberty is rekindled adolescent turmoil must be recognised and the patient will need intensive support" (Crisp, 1983, p. 857).

Treatment

There are different levels and phases to treatment for eating disorders, and how these develop will depend very much on the severity of the condition and the course it takes. If there is significant weight loss or other severe physiological symptoms then some aspects of treatment will almost certainly need to take place outside of the counselling setting. However, it is important that clients be offered the opportunity to access psychological therapy alongside any medical treatment and monitoring of weight and nutrition, in order to help them cope with any weight restoration and it's emotional implications.

There are a variety of approaches to working with eating disorders, ranging from individual therapy with the child or young person, to systemic work with family members alongside the client. Bruch (1973) sees the goal of therapy with eating disorders as enabling the client to gain a sense of their own capabilities and resources rather than for the therapist to replay the role of being somehow the one who knows the answers. For Bruch (1973), a therapist who presents themselves as "knowing"; "… represents in a painful way a repetition of the significant interaction between patient and parents, where 'mother always knew how I felt', with the implication that they themselves do not know how they feel" (Bruch, 1973, p. 336). According to Bruch (1973), "The therapeutic goal is to make it possible for a patient to uncover his own abilities, his resources and inner capacities for thinking, judging, and feeling" (Bruch, 1973, pp. 338–339).

When work is undertaken with the family of a client with an eating disorder it must be done with particular sensitivity to the family dynamics. The family may be very shocked and distressed by the "illness" in their midst and, if they have avoided conflict within their family dynamics, they may feel they do not have the skills to cope with their child's angry feelings and/or behaviour and may try to suppress or control it once again. Crisp (1983) refers to the importance of how the work of the therapy is managed within the family context;

> Subsequent psychotherapy will concentrate on encouraging the anorectic to leave behind her entrapped and childlike role. If this is to occur, personal growth must be promoted and be acceptable to parents and others, so that there is no rupture of primitive bonds or failure to sustain relationships. (Crisp, 1983, p. 857)

It is therefore important that the client be enabled to develop their own sense of resources and capabilities within their existing family relationships if possible. It may be important for the therapy to include some family work in order to for this to occur.

Deliberate self-harm and self-mutilation

Similarly to eating disorders there is a spectrum of self-harming behaviours which are encountered in therapeutic work with both adults and children. At one end are those who attempt or complete a suicidal act with a clear intent to end their life. This will be discussed later in this chapter. According to research (Messer & Fremouw, 2008), adolescent suicide is a relatively rare occurrence while, at the other end of the spectrum, self-mutilating behaviours have a much higher occurrence in an adolescent population (Hawton, Rodham & Evans, 2006).

For practitioners working with self-mutilation, as with eating disorders, there can be some degree of anxiety and confusion regarding what might constitute significant risk of harm and potentially require a breach of confidentiality. Much of the recent research into self-mutilating behaviour amongst adolescents has focussed on an attempt to differentiate clearly between this and suicidal behaviour. It is when this distinction fails to be made either by health care professionals or by family, friends, or teachers, that anxiety can rise and drastic attempts made to curtail the behaviour, running risk of making it worse and certainly making it difficult for dialogue to occur with the self-harmer to try to make meaning of their behaviour. In a paper offering a critical review of self-mutilating behaviours in adolescents, Messer and Fremouw (2008) offer the following characteristics of self-mutilation as defined by research in the field; "… deliberateness, tissue damage without intent to die, social unacceptability, and typical repetitiveness" (Messrs & Fremouw, 2008, p. 164). It is clearly of great importance here to understand that there is no intent to die in the act of self-mutilation by the adolescent and, in that respect, it differs greatly from a suicidal act where there is suicidal ideation alongside an intent to end life.

Having established that young self-mutilating clients are not generally intending to end their lives, it can be possible to begin to work with them in therapy and try to help the client to make sense of their actions and to develop alternative means of managing difficult emotional states.

Often young people who deliberately self-harm can feel anxious about discussing it in their counselling. They may expect a reaction of shock or of contempt along with possible judgement of their behaviour as "attention seeking". As Skegg (2005) points out in an article in the medical journal, *The Lancet*, self-harm is something doctors and other medical staff have particular problems reacting sympathetically to; "… when patients deliberately inflict harm on themselves by, for example, taking overdoses or cutting themselves, the contract between doctor and patient is severely tested" (Skegg, 2005, p. 1471). Given that young people who self-harm may have already met with a negative response from those to whom they disclose or who discover the behaviour, it is even more important that counsellors and therapists are able to convey a different attitude and respond to the disclosure in a way which hopefully encourages understanding.

Significant harm and confidentiality

Whether self-harming behaviours are part of the reason for the referral, or emerge during the course of the therapy, it is vital for practitioners to be able to refer to their original contract and agreement around confidentiality, if they are to be able to offer a safe and boundaried container for the exploration of the issues underlying the behaviour. Clients who are sixteen and over, or who can be deemed to have capacity to consent, are entitled to confidentiality regarding disclosure of self-harm where they are not putting themselves or another at significant risk of harm. Where clients have disclosed self-harm, practitioners are advised to consider, with their client if possible, whether disclosing to another would be in their best interest or not (Bond & Mitchels, 2008). This may be something which changes as the therapy proceeds, particularly if the counsellor becomes concerned that the behaviour is increasing in severity, or if wounds are not being cared for and there is a possible risk of serious infection.

With clients who are not considered to have the capacity to consent to confidentiality it may be advisable to share information regarding self-harm with someone with parental responsibility for the client as a matter of course, in order to ensure the wellbeing of the child.

As long as both practitioner and client are clear about the limits of confidentiality regarding self-harm, it should be possible for trust to develop, allowing for the behaviour to be safely explored as part of the therapeutic work and understood in terms of meaning for each individual client.

Parents and self-harming clients

Self-harm can be an area where there may be a conflict of agenda for the therapy between client, therapist, and parent(s). For many parents who refer their child for counselling having discovered that they are self-harming, the purpose of the therapy is to stop their child from further self-harming behaviour and therefore relieve their anxiety regarding their child's behaviour. Clearly it is distressing to find that your child is making deliberate attempts to damage themselves, and for many parents it can be hard to distinguish between the self-harm and a suicide attempt, resulting in understandably high levels of parental distress. Parents may be very clear that the role of the therapist is to help their child to stop cutting themselves or using other means of self-mutilation. Although therapist and client may also have a goal of eventually being able to relinquish the behaviour, they may see this as the result of first developing an understanding, and then finding other ways to meet the needs currently being supported by the behaviour. Some clinicians (Levenkron, 2006; Selekman, 2006), see communication within the family, and particularly between the self-harming child and their parents as significant in both the development of the symptom and its treatment. Levenkron (2006) writes that; "The parental relationship proves to be a major influence in fostering such harmful behaviour. A second major element is the deficit, or shortage, of genuine communication between other family members and the self-harming child" (Levenkron, 2006, p. 125). In this respect, self-harming behaviours could be understood as an expression of emotions, not adequately taken up and contained by the family environment while the young person was developing. In common once again with eating disorders, it can be important and useful to work alongside parents if possible in enabling the young person to communicate their feelings, and for the parents to be able to receive them. For Selekman (2006), family cohesion and parental presence in the lives of adolescent children are strong determinants of whether children will become self-harmers and also of whether treatment will be successful. He writes;

> The more parents can consistently make themselves available for emotional connection, support their adolescent's strivings for more independence, and provide and enforce rules and their consequences, the less likely their son or daughter will be to engage in self-harming and similar behaviours. (Selekman, 2006, p. x)

Of course, many young people who self-harm and who present for counselling will not want their parents to be involved in the therapeutic work to this extent, and it is important that this is respected by practitioners and that family work is not insisted upon where it is absolutely refused by the client.

Case example—Rory

Rory is a fourteen-year-old boy who has been referred for counselling because his parents believe he could be depressed. Rory has recently become isolated from his friends and spends his time in his room at home listening to music. Rory is not interested in his schoolwork and his grades have dropped, raising concerns among his teachers also. At the therapy assessment, his parents mention that recently Rory's paternal grandfather, whom he was very close to, has died after a long illness.

After two counselling sessions focusing on the loss of his grandfather, Rory breaks down and discloses to his counsellor that he has burnt his arm with a lighter on several occasions during the last month. Rory tells her that he hates himself for doing it and that he had promised himself he would never do something so stupid again. He is only telling his counsellor because he feels so weak for not being able to stop himself and now he doesn't know what to do. Rory says he can't bear for his parents to know because then they will hate him and think that he is stupid too.

Rory's counsellor asks if he will show her the burns, which he does. There are several distinct marks on his left arm which appear to be healing and there is no sign of any infection in the wounds. As Rory is an intelligent child of fourteen his counsellor makes the assessment that he does have the capacity to consent to confidentiality in their therapeutic relationship. She suggests to Rory that in the future it might be helpful for them to share with his parents how he is feeling but that for now she respects his wish to maintain confidentiality. She suggests however that this can only be on the basis that Rory lets her know when he has felt the need to injure himself and that he allows her to see what he has done and to check that there is no danger of infection or other significant harm.

Having agreed to these terms, Rory's counsellor invites him to begin to talk about how he was feeling when he felt the need to burn himself.

In this example the counsellor makes the decision that confidentiality can be maintained at this point but only in an environment where new injuries are disclosed. Individual therapists will have their own strategies and policies for working with self-harming clients but this may be an area where there is a need to re-contract and change the therapeutic frame somewhat to take account of the potential for the client causing themselves significant physical harm. Levenkron (2006) takes the view that if the therapist regularly inspects any damage inflicted, the self-harming client may be less inclined to continue to self-harm as it will no longer be a private act. Levenkron suggests that; "This observation, when done consistently, creates the anticipatory sense of loss of privacy" (Levenkron, 2006, p. 182). He goes on to emphasise the importance of the therapist working alongside a doctor where appropriate rather than take on responsibilities for caring medically for wounds which are beyond the therapist's professional capabilities. By preparing a policy for work with self-mutilating clients, practitioners will be able to convey a confidence in working with this group which can be therapeutic in itself. It is important to bear in mind that if the client is no longer able to self-harm in private they may substitute it for another, potentially harmful, behaviour. With this substitution in mind, Levenkron (2006) writes;

> Again, the personality of the therapist is critical here. The goal of this process is to have the self-mutilator relinquish her privacy and isolation for something more attractive-the connection to another person. This connection has to be safer, more secure, than the patient has experienced for a long time. The criterion of the security of the connection is how much self-harming behaviour is exchanged for talk about feelings. (Levenkron, 2006, p. 183)

The previous case example is a demonstration of this method of working with self-mutilating clients. The counsellor in the example makes it clear to Rory that the self-harming behaviours he has been engaging in are understandable and able to be worked with but that there must be clear boundaries between them in order for this to be possible. The incidents must be shared in counselling and no longer be a private act which only he knows about. She also shows Rory that she is aware he will have had feelings at the time he burned himself and at other times and that she is interested in hearing about these and helping him to understand them. In this way the counsellor is helping Rory to see that his feelings can be spoken about and tolerated by someone else. Often this is an aspect of relationships with which self-mutilators are unfamiliar and which may be why they are drawn to self-harm in the first place.

Substance misuse and risk

Drinking alcohol and experimenting recreationally with drugs are a familiar and almost expected part of teenage behaviour in modern Western culture and one that need not necessarily be pathologised or seen as automatically placing young people at risk of harm (Mirza & Mirza, 2008). Here we are concerned with situations in therapy when children and young peoples' use of drugs and alcohol are such that they represent a risk of significant harm. Details and stories of experimentation with drugs and alcohol may be brought by the young person to their counselling sessions where they can be thought about by client and therapist together in a non-judgemental environment. Counsellors who are told about behaviour around drugs and alcohol by their client need to hold the balance between maintaining confidentiality on the basis of their right to privacy, while endeavouring to ensure that the client is not placing themselves in danger through their behaviour, as well as helping clients to understand any legal implications of their behaviour, where relevant.

Much of how a counsellor reacts to information regarding drug and alcohol use will depend on the age of the client. Once again the concept of capacity to consent is relevant here as a child not yet deemed "Gillick" competent who is disclosing regular use of drugs or alcohol should be raising concerns for the counsellor in terms of child protection. In these cases the counsellor needs to take steps to ensure the safety of the child before beginning to examine any underlying reasons for their behaviour. In most cases this would involve informing the client's parents or carers and ensuring they were aware of the behaviour and able to keep the child safe from further harm.

With a client over sixteen or considered "Gillick" competent, the situation is different. As already discussed, children in this category have the right to the content of their counselling sessions being treated confidentially. Therefore, if they make disclosures of drug and alcohol use in their therapy these need to be treated as confidential by the counsellor unless "disclosure is justifiable in the public interest and/or for the child's protection or that of others" (Bond & Mitchels, 2011, p. 130). Practitioners are required, in this situation, to make an assessment of the young person's drug or alcohol use and decide along with their clinical supervisor if necessary if this is likely to put them at risk of significant harm.

This raises the important question of what constitutes significant harm in relation to drugs and alcohol. In a paper on adolescent substance misuse, Mirza and Mirza (2008) propose and outline a model; "… to classify the stage of substance misuse in young people, starting with non-use at one end, moving through experimental stage, social stage, at-risk (prodromal) stage, and stage of harmful use to substance dependence at the other end" (Mirza & Mirza, 2008, p. 358). The model they provide allows practitioners to consider where their client may be on the continuum at any point in the therapy and therefore be able to intervene appropriately. It is important to consider whether a young person is at the experimental or social stage, or whether their use has changed and is therefore likely to place them at risk if unattended.

Neurological risks of substance misuse

Given the evidence (Bava & Tapert, 2010; Brown, Tapert, Granholm & Delis, 2000) that alcohol and recreational drug misuse in adolescence can have a significant effect on brain development and cognitive functioning, it would appear that adolescents are at an increased risk from the effects of substance misuse in this respect. Although many adolescents may be physically "adult-sized" and feel that they can function and behave as adults, evidence suggests that they are going through profound neurological developments (Cozolino, 2006; Wilkinson, 2006). Although knowledge of the harmful effects of substance misuse on the adolescent brain could usefully be shared with clients in a psycho-educative form, it is, however, unlikely to be considered a basis for breaching confidentiality unless significant harm were indicated by high levels of misuse. Therapists working with clients who are regularly using substances may need to stay alert to any signs of cognitive or other difficulties in this respect. Clients who appear to demonstrate such dysfunctions may require referral to other services.

Other risks from substance misuse

Alongside the more pragmatic risk of getting into trouble with the police, clients who drink heavily or misuse substances could be considered at risk in other respects. Physical and cognitive vulnerability due to alcohol or substance misuse can place young people at increased risk of sexual or violent assault (Kalmakis, 2010; Pape, 2014; Sabri, Coohey & Campbell, 2012). If a young person discloses behaviour in their counselling sessions which indicates that they are not able to keep themselves safe from sexual or physical harm while intoxicated, then that may constitute a safeguarding issue which the counsellor may want to pass on, either to other relevant professionals or to the young person's parents. If a young person is adamant that they do not want to let their parents know about their behaviour, it is possible they will allow a referral to either their GP or a local drugs agency as an alternative. In Britain, local authorities are responsible for the commissioning of agencies to support young people affected by substance misuse. This will often be in the form of a Young Persons Substance Misuse Service (YPSMS) which will provide information for young people and the professionals working with them as well as accept referrals for support and treatment where young people fall within their criteria.

Substance misuse and mental health

Another important risk factor when working with young people who are using substances is the impact this can have on their mental health. Often therapists find themselves encountering young people in their practice who are using alcohol, cannabis, and other substances to manage their depression or anger. This kind of self-medicating behaviour can have major implications for mental health, including the onset or exacerbation of psychosis and other psychiatric disorders in young people (Mirza & Mirza, 2008; Tucker, 2009; Wade et al., 2006). Mirza and Mirza (2008) make the claim in their paper that; "Co existing substance misuse has implications for the onset, clinical course, treatment compliance, and prognosis in young people with psychiatric disorders" (Mirza & Mirza, 2008, p. 358), indicating that this is an issue therapists cannot ignore in terms of the effect substance misuse can potentially have on the progress and outcome of therapeutic work in general. As mentioned previously, it can be useful for counsellors of young people to use local young people's substance misuse services along with their own clinical supervision as points of reference and guidance when making an assessment of harm in relation to a client's substance misuse.

Case example—Peter

Peter is a fifteen-year-old boy being seen by a therapist in private practice. He has been referred by his parents due to their concern that he might be depressed. As the therapy continues Peter begins to talk about his use of cannabis. At first he talks about this as something he does occasionally at the weekend but not to excess. Peter's dad has confronted him about it as he has read articles in the press suggesting that smoking cannabis may be contributing to his son's depression. Peter tells the therapist that he reacted defensively to his dad but that he realises that he may be right in what he says. He began smoking because it seemed to lift his mood and distance him from some of his negative thoughts but now he is experiencing some increasingly negative side effects. Peter discloses that he has been smoking regularly on his own, often on the way to school in the morning and after school in his room. This is because, he says, it had been helping him to cope with the difficulty of being in school and home alone in the evenings. Now Peter is finding that his low-mood is worsening at times and that he is struggling to engage academically at school, which is raising his anxiety levels considerably.

Peter's therapist recognises that this indicates a change in use from the social and experimental smoking with friends at the weekend, to something which could potentially be more harmful if ignored. The therapist discusses this with Peter and they agree that something has changed and begin to explore what this might be, initially by thinking about what Peter is struggling with in school and at home in the evenings.

In this example we see that the therapist is considering what place Peter's substance misuse has in his life as well as what part it might be playing in his other difficulties. The therapist is willing to change his approach to Peter's substance use when he recognises a change in Peter's relationship with cannabis. Here we can see the importance of the therapist's attitude and the therapeutic alliance in creating a space where Peter feels safe enough to talk openly with his therapist about his substance use.

Therapy is not a place for judgement of behaviour but a place where clients can discover their own relationship with their behaviours and also feel safe that if necessary someone is maintaining boundaries that will protect them.

Sexual behaviours and risk

Adolescence is a time in young peoples' lives when romantic relationships are becoming increasingly significant and play an important role in identity development (Erikson, 1968; Furman & Shaffer, 2003). For most adolescents, early romantic and sexual relationships are part of their general developmental shift away from prioritising family connections to building their own relationships and attachments within their peer group. Although for many young people negotiating these relationships can cause pain and turmoil, it is nonetheless far from being pathological. However, this can be an area where practitioners become concerned that young people are possibly at risk, particularly with regard to their sexual behaviour. According to Furman and Shaffer (2003); "The development of sexuality is another key task in adolescence. As adolescents' bodies begin to mature in reproductive capacities, their sexual desires increase" (Furman & Shaffer, 2003, p. 10). Practitioners may find that children and young people will bring their early sexual experiences into their counselling sessions to explore as part of their therapy. As in earlier sections of this chapter, the question for the practitioner here is how to know when these exploratory behaviours may represent risk of significant harm for the client. Sexual behaviours have always had an element of risk to them for young people (Cook, Erdman & Dickens, 2007; Kotchik, Shaffer & Forehand, 2001). Sexual intercourse brings with it the risk of unwanted pregnancy, and all physical sexual contact has potential health risks including sexually transmitted diseases. A more recent concern regarding the sexual behaviour of children and young people has been that involving internet and smartphone technology and, in particular, the relatively new phenomena of "sexting", defined in the following by Ringrose, Gill, Livingstone, and Harvey (2012); "Sexting has been conventionally defined as 'exchange of sexual messages or images' and 'the creating, sharing and forwarding of sexually suggestive nude or nearly nude images' through mobile phones and/or the internet" (Ringrose, Gill, Livingstone & Harvey, 2012, p. 6). Therapists may increasingly hear concerning tales of clients and their friends sharing explicit images of each other via mobile phone technology.

The question to be considered is when does sexual experimentation and exploration place someone at risk of significant harm? As in previous sections, answering this question often demands close attention from practitioners to the material presented during sessions, in order that the client's right to confidentiality be protected without putting them at risk of danger or abuse. In this respect, the concept of capacity to consent is once more of considerable importance. If a child is aged thirteen or under, then any physically sexual relationship they enter into will be a criminal matter and prosecutable under The Sexual Offences Act (HM Government, 2003). If they are older than this, there are considerably more grey areas for therapists to negotiate. Although young people who are over sixteen or deemed "Gillick" competent have the right to confidential guidance on sexual matters, the Department of Health is clear that this is not an absolute;

> Where a health professional believes that there is a risk to the health, safety or welfare of a young person or others which is so serious as to outweigh the young person's right to privacy, they should follow locally agreed child protection protocols … In these circumstances, the over-riding objective must be to safeguard the young person. (HM Government (DofH), 2004, p. 3)

Some researchers (Werkele & Avgoustus, 2003) argue that young people who have experienced maltreatment and insecure attachments in childhood are likely to carry these problems into their adolescent and adult romantic and sexual relationships, with the potentially risky consequences of; "showing an accelerated push towards dating (i.e., early age of onset), as well as prematurely transferring priority attachment from caregivers to their partners" (Werkele & Avgoustus, 2003, p. 214).

If this is the case, then that particular type of young person may be entering into sexual relationships at an age when they may not be ready to cope with the pressures they bring and may lack the support of family relationships as well. This may lead to an increase of risk of their being coerced into having sex as well as taking risks with their sexual health and protection from pregnancy. The following case example shows how a practitioner might manage their concerns in this area.

Case example—Lauren

Lauren is a fourteen-year-old girl being seen in private practice. Her father, who is raising her alone, originally referred her for counselling due to concerns regarding her angry and violent outbursts, often directed towards him around boundary setting.

Lauren has been seeing her counsellor for about six months when she begins to talk in sessions about a new boyfriend, Liam, she has started seeing. He is in year twelve in the sixth form at the same school where Lauren is in year nine. Lauren tells the counsellor that her dad does not know she is seeing him and she is afraid if he finds out he will stop her. It is clear to the counsellor that Liam is very important to Lauren, who struggles to maintain a positive self-image, but the counsellor is concerned that Lauren is seeing an older boy without her father's knowledge.

Lauren would be considered "Gillick" competent and, as she is adamant that she does not want her dad to know at this point, her counsellor feels she has a duty to maintain her confidentiality. A few sessions later Lauren tells her counsellor that she has had sex with Liam and that they did not use a condom as he didn't have one with him. Lauren says that she was very scared about being pregnant so she managed to convince a friend to go with her to the family planning clinic to get the morning after pill. The nurse there wanted her to think about the contraceptive pill as well as having a test for chlamydia. Lauren says she hasn't discussed this with Liam as she "doesn't want him to think that she is a baby". When the counsellor asks if Lauren has talked about what happened with Liam with any other adults she says, no, there is no one she feels she can talk to who wouldn't tell her dad.

After the session Lauren's counsellor feels some concern that Lauren may be at further risk from her relationship with Liam and her sexual activity generally. She discusses the content of the session with her clinical supervisor at their next session. Her supervisor agrees that there are concerns regarding this relationship for Lauren, but says that there are currently no grounds for breaching confidentiality. Lauren has the right to privacy and to receive guidance as regards contraception and sexually transmitted diseases without her parent's explicit knowledge. They agree that it is useful that Lauren feels able to be open about her relationship in the sessions and that it is in the best interests of her therapy to do so and therefore be able to begin to think about the implications of the relationship. In supervision, they discuss both the practical implications of the sexual relationship in terms of safeguarding, as well as considering Lauren's apparent transference of her intimacy needs onto this older boy. Both counsellor and supervisor agree that the counsellor needs to be sure that Lauren is able to think clearly about how to keep herself safe in the relationship if confidentiality is to be maintained.

Very often young people can find it difficult to communicate with parents about sexual feelings and relationships. As Cook, Erdman, and Dickens (2007) point out, this can lead to conflict between young people and their families in this area;

> Parents who have reared their adolescent children from birth and remain familiar with their earlier childish behavior and immature or innocent judgements may be slow to recognize their children's emerging sexuality and evolving capacity to make their own choices, and to bear responsibility for their own choices. (Cook, Erdman & Dickens, 2007, p. 182)

This means that counselling can become an important space for young people to explore their developing sexuality with a concerned adult, in an atmosphere which respects their development in this area in ways which might be more difficult for parents. Confidentiality is important in this respect, and the law is clear in this respect that young people under sixteen should be given access to confidential guidance and advice regarding their sexual and reproductive health. Once again however, this confidentiality is not absolute, as outlined in the guidance from the Department of Health (2004) mentioned previously.

Online sexual behaviour and risk

As mentioned previously in this chapter, therapists may also be concerned about the risks that clients may be exposed to through their sexual behaviour online. There has been growing concern in the last few years amongst professionals, parents, and the general public regarding the vulnerability of children and young people to online sexual abuse, and there have been many cases where paedophiles have been found to target and groom vulnerable children online (Kloess, Beech & Harkins, 2014; McCartan & McAlister, 2012). If a counsellor were to become concerned that a client was perhaps being groomed in such a way or seemed to be vulnerable due to their online behaviour they would need to treat this in accordance with all safeguarding concerns and act according to their child protection policy.

There have been concerns raised in the media recently regarding the phenomenon of "sexting", and this is something which young people may raise in their therapy sessions. As defined earlier in the chapter, "sexting" is the sharing of explicit material via mobile technology or social networks and media. In their recent qualitative study into "sexting" for the NSPCC, Ringrose, Gill, Livingstone, and Harvey (2012) explore and discuss in depth the phenomenon and its implications. Most importantly they suggest that for professionals involved in the welfare of children; "… inquiring about the possible implication of online/mobile technologies should now be routine" (Ringrose, Gill, Livingstone & Harvey, 2012, p. 59). Practitioners should be as interested in client's online social networks and behaviours as they are in their relationships at school and home. As "sexting" involves the sharing of often explicit images, there have been cases both in the UK and the USA of young people being prosecuted under laws associated with indecent images. As McCartan and McAllister (2012) point out;

> … many young people are unaware that publishing a photo of someone under 18 years of age, that is of a sexual nature, is illegal. Therefore, when young people upload sexually provocative images of them online or share such images via their mobile phones, they are, technically breaking the law. (McCartan & McAllister, 2012, p. 263)

As it is only recently that children and young people have engaged in sexual behaviours online, it is sometimes difficult for professionals to feel fully confident in this area. Young people are often unaware not only of the law surrounding "sexting" but also of the risks in terms of the consequences of their actions. They are not necessarily aware until too late of how they will feel if their image is shared beyond the person it was intended for, or how vulnerable sharing explicit images can render them. This is something they can be assisted in thinking about in their therapy sessions. There is also a difference between voluntary and coercive "sexting", and Simpson (2013) suggests in the following; "… that there may well be an important distinction between coerced sexting and those situations where a young person sends their own image to others as part of their sex play within a relationship" (Simpson, 2013, pp. 699–700). Practitioners need to be particularly attentive to anything in the client's material that indicates they are being coerced into sexual behaviour online, and use their safeguarding policy and clinical supervision to consider this, while respecting their right to a private sexual life. Sexual experimentation is becoming increasingly popular amongst young people online and McCartan and McAllister (2012) quote research from 2009 demonstrating that; … one in five teens have sent or posted semi nude or nude images of them in cyberspace" (McCartan & McAllister, 2012, p. 263). Online sexual behaviour of all kinds is not something that young people are going to cease simply because adults are shocked or angered by it. Practitioners need to hold the line in this area between understanding that children and young people are likely to continue to behave sexually via technology and will want to explore this in their therapy, and being attentive to when this behaviour is placing them at risk of significant harm. As Ringrose, Gill, Livingstone, and Harvey (2012) suggest; "… despite the anxieties that the worst cases can provoke, these professionals too must recognise and allow for children's legitimate opportunities to develop and express their sexuality in privacy and dignity" (Ringrose, Gill, Livingstone & Harvey, 2012, p. 60). Once again, in this respect clinical supervision and training in this new and complex field are of great value to the practitioner.

Mental health issues and risk

So far, this chapter has examined instances of risk where the young person struggling with the developmental demands of adolescence develops a symptom or behaviour such as an eating disorder or issue with substance misuse which may well become the focus of their therapy for some time. For other young people it is their mood, and/or their thoughts and cognitions which can put them at risk if these difficulties are not recognised by family, or professionals.

This section will consider when depression and other mood disorders, as well as distortions in cognition and perception, can place children at risk of significant harm.

Depression and risk

Many children seen for counselling might be considered to show signs of depression and low-mood and practitioners may feel relatively comfortable working with such presentations within their general practice. However, there are occasions where low-mood can become entrenched, and chronic, along with a profound sense of hopelessness, leading some children to attempt and possibly complete suicide. Laufer (1997), writing about adolescent breakdown, suggests that the question here for professionals; "… can be summarized as follows: how do we know when to be worried, and when is help urgent?" (Laufer, 1997, p. 3).

In many respects practitioners will be looking for the same signs of risk in young clients as they might when working with adults with depression. In therapeutic work with children who are experiencing some form of depression or low-mood it is important to carry out an assessment of the risk of them harming themselves. There are various ways that this can be carried out. Those practitioners wishing to make a formal assessment might choose to use CORE (Clinical Outcomes in Routine Evaluation) (Mellor-Clark, Barkham, Connell & Evans, 1999), possibly adapted for use with children and adolescents. There are also other evaluation tools available such as the Beck Depression Inventory (BDI), Beck Hopelessness Scale (BHS) and the Beck Scale for Suicidal Ideation (BSS) (Cochrane-Brink, Lofchy & Sakinofsky, 2000) which may be useful for practitioners to be aware of.

Perhaps the most useful tool in this respect possessed by the therapist, is the therapeutic relationship itself. Once this is established and the client has developed trust in the counsellor it may be possible to detect from the client's narrative and presentation if there is any increase in risk factors which could possibly lead to a suicide attempt. If a counsellor is concerned that their client has become increasingly isolated from friends and family, is less able to experience and express a sense of hope and of a future or if they have actively begun to speak about a wish to die, there should be concerns that the client may be at risk of seriously harming themselves. In these circumstances the counsellor would need to discuss their concerns initially with the client and then decide, hopefully together, what the best course of action will be. In all cases where such action is deemed necessary, consent to breach confidentiality should be sought, but if not granted and a counsellor has serious concerns regarding the client's safety and wellbeing, they must pass these concerns on to the relevant services. Likewise, if a counsellor is working with a young person who attempts suicide while in therapy, then a full risk assessment should be carried out before therapy resumes. The following chapter on referring on and working with other services will examine this process in more depth.

Psychosis and thought disorders

Psychosis and thought disorders are rare in general, but can sometimes emerge during adolescence (Lee & Jureidini, 2013; Marks Mishne, 1986). As discussed earlier in this chapter, symptoms of psychosis may be experienced by clients who have engaged in substance misuse (Lee, & Jureidini 2013; Tucker, 2009) and practitioners should always try to establish if this has been the case as part of their assessment of the symptoms. The symptoms experienced and described by a client that might indicate psychosis are outlined in a recent report by the British Psychological Society (BPS) in the following;

> These experiences include hearing voices ("hallucinations"), believing things that others find strange ("delusions"), speaking in a way that others find hard to follow ("thought disorder") and experiencing periods of confusion where you appear out of touch with reality ("acute psychosis"). (British Psychological Society, 2014, p. 10)

These signs on their own may not indicate psychosis or schizophrenia and do not necessarily indicate that a client requires medication or psychiatric intervention. The BPS (2014) report indicates that talking therapies can be very useful in the treatment of these symptoms, particularly in allowing clients to develop their own understanding of their symptoms and their meaning, rather than being immediately medically diagnosed and prescribed drug treatments. For some, these symptoms occur as a result of trauma or maltreatment in the past and therapy can offer an important space for this to be explored. However, in terms of risk with regard to these symptoms in young people, therapists may wish to consult with a child and adolescent psychiatrist or with local NHS CAMHS in order to be supported in deciding how to proceed.

Summary

- Practitioners must be prepared to encounter risk in therapeutic work with children and young people.
- Risk must be assessed as to whether it is likely to lead to "significant harm" to the client or another.
- The therapeutic boundaries must be established in such a way to allow issues to be explored in confidence but also to protect clients from significant harm.
- Practitioners may need to consider referring on or working alongside other professionals if the client's needs are beyond the scope of what can be provided by the therapy in isolation.

PART III

PROFESSIONAL ISSUES IN PRIVATE PRACTICE WITH CHILDREN AND YOUNG PEOPLE

CHAPTER SEVEN

Referring on and working with other agencies

As outlined in chapter six, there are occasions during the course of therapy when a client requires an intervention or some further support which may fall beyond the scope of the practitioner they are currently working with. This could be for a number of reasons; a practitioner may find for example that a client's eating issues have worsened and now require specialist intervention, or a young person they have been working with for a while discloses that they have been hearing voices. If circumstances such as these arise, then a consultation with another service should be considered by the practitioner. This could mean that a client is referred on to another professional or agency and that their therapy sessions end, or it may mean a shift to multidisciplinary working where therapy or counselling is one of a range of interventions being offered.

This chapter explores these processes in depth, including examining when an onward referral may be necessary, what form this might take, as well as how this might impact on the client and the therapy already being undertaken.

Practising within ethical limits

The BACP *Ethical Framework* (2013) states that;

> 2. Practitioners should give careful consideration to the limits of their training and experience and work within these limits, taking advantage of available professional support. (BACP, 2013, p. 4)

Similarly, the UKCP code of professional conduct (2009) includes the following clauses;

> 5.3 The psychotherapist commits to recognise the boundaries and limitations of their expertise and techniques and to take the necessary steps to maintain their ability to practice competently.
>
> 5.4 If it becomes clear that a case is beyond a psychotherapist's scope of practice, the psychotherapist commits to inform the client and where appropriate offer an alternative psychotherapist or other professional where requested. (UKCP, 2009, p. 6)

These clauses draw attention to the fact that, on occasion, issues arise in the therapeutic process which are beyond the scope of practitioners to manage within their own practice, and which require either professional support or an onward referral. It is the responsibility of practitioners in this situation to ensure that any onward referral or multidisciplinary work is carried out with the best interest of the client in mind, including their right to confidentiality if applicable.

Primary care referrals and communication

When a counsellor recognises during the course of therapy, or even at assessment, an aspect of the work which seems beyond their scope, they may seek a referral for the child or young person to another service. In the first instance this may be primary health care services, principally the client's GP and primary care clinic. Practitioners may choose to make the referral themselves in consultation with the client, or they may suggest that the client or their parents make an appointment themselves. This will depend on the age of the child and the nature of the referral. Where a counsellor themselves makes the referral to the GP, it is important that any communication is made with the consent of the client, unless this is not possible. The communication should contain a clear and succinct outline of the issues, state clearly the nature and duration of the therapeutic relationship with the client, and communicate to the professional what information regarding the referral has been shared with the client. This may be in the form of an explicit statement that the communication has been seen and agreed upon by the client.

Child and Adolescent Mental Health Services (CAMHS)

One of the initial places where practitioners might look for support in cases where they feel an onward referral due to a mental health issue may be necessary, are the local CAMHS. CAMHS are specialist NHS services offering support to children and young people up to age eighteen and their families, as well advice and consultation to other professionals working with this group. There are a range of professionals employed by CAMHS including child and adolescent psychiatrists, psychotherapists, family therapists, nurses, social workers, and psychologists, amongst others. Many CAMHS also employ mental health workers and support workers to engage with children and their families at a lower intensity than a psychiatrist or psychologist might. The way CAMHS works and what is offered to whom can vary enormously from locality to locality, so it is important that private practitioners have a good knowledge of what is offered to children and families in their particular local area and how to access it. CAMHS services are divided according to tiers indicating the type and severity of problem and the professionals who work with them. The table below (8.1) outlines the type of support offered by NHS CAMHS at each tier and who is likely to deliver it:

This table suggests that a counsellor in private practice who has a concern regarding a child or young person's mental health, and is seeking consultation with a CAMHS specialist, would be advised to make contact at the tier two level. Many local UK CAMHS services offer "guidance to referrers" documents as well as helplines to assist professionals and members of the public in making appropriate referrals to CAMHS. They may also have their own website offering local referral information as well as guidance on accessing other available services for young people locally. Local Authority Children's' Services websites can also be useful in this respect. Community CAMHS also often have

Table 8.1. Outline of NHS CAMHS four tier strategic framework (HM Government, DFCS, Every Child Matters, 2010).

Tier	Delivered by	Services offered
1.	Practitioners who are not specialist mental health workers, i.e. GP's, nurses, social workers, school nurses.	General advice offered to try to manage less severe problems or referral made to a higher tier service.
2.	Practitioners who are generally CAMHS specialists working in community and primary care settings, i.e. primary mental health workers, psychologists, and counsellors.	Consultation to families and practitioners working with children and young people in other settings. Assessment of children and families possibly leading to treatment at another tier.
3.	Multi-disciplinary teams including child and adolescent psychiatrists, clinical psychologists, child and adolescent psychotherapists, family therapists, occupational therapists, community psychiatric nurses, art, music and drama therapists.	More specialised services for children and their families where more complex, severe or persistent disorders have been identified during assessment.
4.	Highly specialised out-patient teams or in-patient units including a variety of specialised and highly trained mental health practitioners.	Specialised interventions and support for those children and young people with the most complex and severe issues. These can include eating disorder services, forensic adolescent units, and psychiatric services amongst others.

links in to other services operated for young children in the locality, such as drug and alcohol support, eating disorders and early intervention for psychosis. It can be very useful for therapists to have up-to-date knowledge of which services are operating locally to them, as well as details of how they, or their clients, can access them.

One route into CAMHS services in the UK is via the client's GP. In some cases it is appropriate to suggest to parents, after consultation with the client, that an appointment is made at their surgery to discuss any concerns, and seek a referral themselves via the child's GP. In most cases it will be important that the child or young person continues to receive counselling whilst they are awaiting the outcome of any CAMHS referral.

Alongside, or as an alternative to NHS CAMHS there are many private medical organisations who also offer a CAMHS provision. Similarly to the NHS, accessing their services will often require a referral from the child's GP and then assessment by a child and adolescent psychiatrist, after which, different options for treatment will be proposed or suggestions made as to what course to follow next. Often private CAMHS providers offer their own talking therapies "in-house", and they may suggest that clients have therapy with one of their therapists as part of any treatment plan they provide. It is important that the referring practitioner is involved in this process, alongside their client, in order to achieve the most beneficial outcome. Sometimes it may be useful for the client to pause their counselling while they undergo treatment, but it is important to ensure that they are not forced to terminate a therapeutic relationship with which they are comfortable and familiar if it is not in their best interests to do so.

Consultation

While it may not be necessary or appropriate for every client to be referred to and be treated by CAMHS when there are mental health or other concerns, it can be useful for counsellors working in private practice to be able to consult with specialist practitioners from time to time. In adult work it is not uncommon for therapists in private practice to build a relationship and connection with a psychiatrist who is happy to offer professional advice and consultation. This can be equally of use in work with children and young people. A child and adolescent psychiatrist who is happy to be consulted with on mental health and psychiatric concerns could be an important member of a private practitioner's support network. The chapter on training and support will look in more depth at how to cultivate such a network but it might be useful for therapists beginning their private practice with children and adolescents to make contact with CAMHS locally, and to write to local child and adolescent psychiatrists, asking if they would be available for consultation. If such a connection is made this then offers counsellors the option of discussing concerns they may have regarding a child or young person's mental health in confidence, before making a referral into other services.

The following case example will examine how a counsellor manages a consultation and CAMHS referral regarding one of her clients.

Case example—Maggie and Lauren. Part One

Sixteen-year-old Lauren has been seeing her counsellor, Maggie, for about twelve sessions when she discloses in a session that she has been using laxatives and making herself sick regularly, as a way of controlling her weight, since she was thirteen years old. She was initially referred for counselling after her GP suggested to her mum it might be useful due to the severe anxiety attacks she had been experiencing since beginning college in September. Lauren tells Maggie that she is now beginning to be fearful that she is damaging herself physically through her behaviours, but is also anxious that if she is treated for an eating disorder she will no longer be able to control her weight, and will become "fat". Lauren's parents are divorced and she spends half of her week with each of them. Her mum is single and works long hours as a property lawyer, while her father has remarried and has eighteen-month-old twin daughters with his new wife. Maggie asks Lauren if her parents are aware of her issues with eating, and she says that she has managed to keep her use of laxatives and purging hidden from them, although she thinks they might be aware that at times she overeats as her mum and step-mum have both complained about finding food wrappers under her bed and in the clothes basket.

Maggie wonders with Lauren if perhaps there is a part of her that would like her parents to notice that something is wrong, since she has left wrappers where they could be found in her homes. Lauren agrees that this might be the case, and says that for a long time she has felt out of control, but not able to tell anyone how she is feeling.

Maggie and Lauren decide it could be useful to let mum know some of what has been happening around food, and also for Lauren to speak to her GP regarding any physical effects of her behaviour.

Lauren is anxious regarding this, and she and Maggie talk about this as an important part of her coming to terms with what has been going on for her. They agree that this is the start of her dealing with the feelings that are underlying her relationship with food and her body, but that talking to the GP, and facing her fears with her mum's support is an important part of this.

Maggie and Lauren agree for Maggie to make contact with Lauren's mum to discuss what has emerged in the session, and for an appointment with the GP to then be arranged.

This example shows the counsellor responding to what her client has disclosed in different ways. She acknowledges that there is therapeutic work to be done in understanding the underlying cause of Lauren's troubled relationship with food and her body but that, given how long Lauren has been engaging in these behaviours, there is also a need for any potential physical implications to be assessed. Maggie picks up from Lauren's narrative that she seems to want her parents' support with this, and therefore suggests that they involve mum at this stage. In this way Maggie is offering Lauren the security of being able to continue her therapy, but also taking her concerns seriously enough to make sure they are addressed outside of the therapy as well as within it.

If a client in similar circumstances was unwilling for the counsellor to make contact with their parents, they could still be encouraged to make an appointment with their GP. As discussed previously, if a counsellor is concerned that there is the potential risk of significant harm to a child or young person, then there is no longer an automatic duty to maintain confidentiality.

Case example—Maggie and Lauren. Part Two

Maggie contacts Lauren's mum and they discuss Lauren's disclosure of her behaviour around purging and laxatives. Mum is initially shocked and upset, but she also recognises that she had suspicions that this was going on, but because Lauren had always been around a healthy weight, she had not voiced her concerns. They agree that it would be helpful for them to meet up for a review session, and also for mum to arrange a doctor's appointment for Lauren.

Lauren's GP recommends that she is referred to the NHS CAMHS in order to be assessed regarding her potential eating disorder, and also suggests a referral to a paediatrician to assess any physiological or developmental issues Lauren may be experiencing. As mum has private healthcare insurance for herself and Lauren, they decide that they will access CAMHS privately for Lauren's assessment. Maggie suggests that they inform whoever assesses her that Lauren is having counselling, and to give the clinic her contact details. Maggie agrees with Lauren that she will not disclose any information regarding Lauren's counselling sessions without her explicit permission.

Referring on and confidentiality

It is important for therapists to be clear about their duty to maintain confidentiality with regards to information sharing when further referrals are made during the course of counselling. It is clearly useful for professionals who are intending to support a child or young person as part of a team to be aware of each other's involvement. In the UK, since the government report (2003) following the death of Victoria Climbie in February 2000, there has been an even greater emphasis on the importance of professionals sharing information regarding the health and care of children. This is intended to ensure that children receive the best possible care, and are not put at risk. The UK government have published a range of guidelines for practitioners regarding multi-agency working, and the sharing of confidential information, which are helpful resources for counsellors and supervisors to refer to when working with other agencies. Details of these are included in the useful resources section at the back of the book.

It is vital that counsellors continue to maintain their duty of confidentiality regarding the content of their client's sessions, even when other professionals are involved. This can sometimes feel difficult when liaising with professionals who may not necessarily work from the same boundaries regarding confidentiality as counsellors do, and who share more information about the work and the client than perhaps a therapist might. One way to manage a client's concerns regarding confidentiality might be to copy them in to any information which is shared with other professionals via reports or letters. This way, transparency is maintained, protecting the client's right to know what information is being shared and kept about them. In the same way as was outlined regarding reviews with parents, any information likely to be considered confidential, which is to be shared with other agencies, must be agreed to by the client first. In this respect, a client who has been referred on to another agency or professional can maintain a sense of trust in their counsellor as well as in the confidentiality of the therapeutic relationship, at a point when they are likely to be feeling quite vulnerable regarding the transition into other services.

Case example—Maggie and Lauren. Part Three

Maggie continues to meet with Lauren for her weekly counselling sessions while she is waiting to be assessed by a child and adolescent psychiatrist. They talk about Lauren's anxieties regarding the assessment and any possible diagnosis. Lauren tells Maggie that her mum has spoken to her dad about what is happening, and that he is being supportive, although her step-mum accused Lauren of attention seeking because she is jealous of her twin sisters. Lauren was upset by this and expressed to Maggie her own concerns that this might be the case, although is relieved somewhat when Maggie points out that her issues with food and laxatives began before the twins were born.

After the assessment has taken place, Maggie receives a report in the post from the psychiatrist, giving the details of the assessment. Maggie has been copied in to receive this letter along with Lauren's GP and her parents. In the report, the psychiatrist, Dr. Clare Richards, gives a diagnosis of bulimia nervosa and recommends that Lauren receives cognitive behavioural therapy via the eating disorders unit at the clinic, in order to work on her thinking and behaviours around food and her body, while also meeting with Dr. Richards along with her parents regularly to continue to assess the bulimia and its physiological impact on her health. The letter acknowledges that Lauren is currently receiving counselling from a private practitioner, but suggests that this should end while Lauren is undergoing treatment at the clinic for her bulimia. In a covering letter Dr. Richards asks for a report from Maggie regarding the counselling, and suggests that they speak on the phone regarding Lauren as soon as possible.

Maggie does not respond immediately to the report from Dr. Richards, but decides to wait until she has had clinical supervision before taking any action. In her supervision session, Maggie and her clinical supervisor discuss the report, as well as Lauren's ongoing counselling sessions with Maggie. Maggie discusses her concerns about bringing Lauren's sessions to a close at this point when she seems so vulnerable and anxious regarding her treatment, and in need of counselling support as she goes through this transition. They also talk about the issues inherent in having two therapeutic relationships running concurrently. Maggie agrees that it might not be desirable for Lauren to continue with weekly counselling if she is also having cognitive behavioural therapy at the clinic, but she and her supervisor explore the idea of her continuing to meet with Lauren perhaps less frequently as a way of offering supportive counselling during the treatment period. Maggie also uses the space of her supervision to reflect on her misgivings about the care Lauren may receive at the clinic and whether this will be as helpful for her as the counselling Maggie is offering. Maggie and her supervisor agree that it is important to bear in mind what is best for Lauren at this point, and what her wishes are for her continuing treatment.

With this in mind Maggie meets Lauren for their usual session. Lauren uses the space to talk about her experience at the assessment. She speaks positively about Dr. Richards who she says she found easy to talk to. Lauren says that she would like to give the CBT a try as Dr. Richards spoke very positively about it, but she is concerned about not seeing Maggie for support during this time. Lauren says that she thinks that Dr. Richards is focussed on treating her bulimia and, while that is helpful and what she wants, she is worried this will not give her enough space to explore her other feelings, particularly regarding her family and friendships. Maggie and Lauren discuss different options, and talk about why continuing with weekly counselling while the CBT is going on might be difficult and perhaps confusing or overwhelming for Lauren. Maggie suggests that perhaps they could continue to meet, but perhaps less frequently while Lauren is having CBT. They agree that meeting every four weeks would be helpful, and decide to discuss this option with mum and Dr. Richards. Maggie also lets Lauren know that Dr. Richards has asked for a report from her regarding Lauren's counselling. They agree together what should go in this report, and Maggie says that she will copy Lauren in when she sends it to the clinic. They agree to meet again the following week to bring their weekly sessions to an end, just before the CBT is due to begin.

Having agreed this change to the contract with Lauren's mum, Maggie contacts Dr. Richards and they discuss Maggie's proposal. They agree that removing Lauren's counselling with Maggie entirely at this point might be detrimental to her successful treatment, as it might increase her anxiety and reluctance to move away from the bulimic behaviours. They agree to Maggie continuing to meet with Lauren on a monthly basis and for Maggie to receive any reports which come from the clinic, so she is kept informed about Lauren's treatment.

In this case, Maggie and Lauren decide to continue to maintain their therapeutic relationship while she receives outpatient treatment for an eating disorder. Here, potentially, the counselling becomes a way of maintaining Lauren's sense of a secure base, which will continue to be available for her while she is undergoing treatment elsewhere. In this model, the counselling provides one aspect of what is needed by the client and other aspects are provided by the clinic and the GP.

In the example, Maggie speaks in supervision about her misgivings regarding the therapeutic services offered by the clinic and the help her client will potentially receive from them. Such concerns are commonly experienced by therapists when they are managing onward referrals to other agencies. When working with other professionals there can be a risk of some "splitting" occurring where other practitioners are viewed as "bad" and as offering less beneficial treatments. This is possibly a way of the therapist managing the threat to their sense of competence, which may be challenged when there is a need to refer on. If therapists are unaware that this is occurring, it may be that they unconsciously block or sabotage the communication with the other agency, or try to contaminate the work. In this respect, it is important that practitioners work through their potential feelings of rivalry with other practitioners in their own clinical supervision, so that the best interests of the client are maintained. Alternatively, counsellors may be too ready to see other professionals as "experts", and as having more to offer the client than they themselves have. It can be easy for therapists to feel intimidated by the qualifications and supposed expertise of other professionals and, again, this must not be allowed to interfere with providing clients with the treatment which will be of most benefit for them.

Therapists need also to be attentive to any sign that parents or the client are also getting caught in "splitting". This can occur both in terms of client or parents idealising the current therapist and feeling anxious regarding the transition to another service, or vice versa. It is important that, as with their clients, therapists make themselves available as appropriate to allowing parents to openly discuss their feelings regarding onward referrals. Particularly in the case of younger children, parents may experience concern and anxiety regarding the transition to another service or professional, and therapists can be supportive to parents and clients in exploring their concerns with them in an open and constructive manner.

Working with difference in other agencies

Crucial to managing potential "splits" between agencies, is the capacity to understand and manage difference in terms of theoretical orientations and approaches in various services for children and young people. The earlier chapter on working with risk looked in particular at how a therapist in private practice might manage issues of risk presenting in a session. The chapter explored when it might be necessary to breach confidentiality, and when it was possible to contain what was disclosed within the therapeutic relationship. As already established, the boundaries regarding maintaining confidentiality are very different for practitioners in private practice than they are in other agencies, and this is something it is important for a counsellor in private practice to bear in mind when a client is referred into an agency where the policies are likely to be different.

Some agencies for example, will want a child or young person who is using drugs or alcohol to undertake work to address this, either before they begin any other therapy or, at least, alongside it. This can be problematic for young people who have not yet come to the point of seeing their substance misuse as problematic, but who perhaps require help in other areas. This can also create confusion and difficulties for the client and parents when the other agency seems to take a different position on substance misuse than the counsellor in private practice has. Parents may feel vindicated by the response of the new agency or professional, while the young person can feel that their autonomy is being further denied, and they have become marginalised by the transition process. It can be useful, where this looks like being the case, if therapists are able to discuss the differences between agencies and therapists openly with clients and their families.

Clients may also need to be prepared for differences in therapeutic approach where this is changing with the onward referral. This preparation can range from making space for the client to express their anxieties around changing their therapist, to explaining that different people have different ways of working, not necessarily better or worse, and that this can sometimes take some getting used to. Being able to have this kind of conversation during the transition to another service can help clients to understand that they may find that other professionals and services offer a different therapeutic approach than they may have become used to, but that this is not necessarily a negative. This can be beneficial in helping clients to work through any issues they may have regarding coping with change and difference.

Impact on the therapeutic alliance

When a referral to other services occurs during the course of counselling, this is likely to have an impact on the pre-existing therapeutic relationship. This impact will of course vary enormously from situation to situation and therapists need to be attentive and responsive to any manifestations of this in the therapeutic relationship. How any impact is identified and engaged with in the therapy will depend, to some extent, on the therapeutic model employed by individual practitioners. However, it is important that the implications of the onward referral are not ignored, or dismissed defensively, due to the practitioners' fears of a potential attack on their competency, or professional standing. It is important that, if therapy continues alongside a referral to another service, that it remains a safe space for the client to explore all their feelings and responses to those they are working with. Daines, Gask, and Howe (2007) draw attention to both the risks and benefits of onward referrals in *Medical and Psychiatric Issues for Counsellors*; "There are always risks to a referral while a client is engaged in therapeutic work, but the reasons for referral can be to complement treatment as well as to assess physical or psychiatric problems" (Daines, Gask & Howe, 2007, p. 15).

The authors go on to identify potential risks in the following; "The fears of clients that counsellors are rejecting them when referrals are made should be a focus of therapeutic discussion …" (Daines, Gask & Howe, 2007, p. 16).

This discussion could be seen as even more important in the context of work with children and young people, where there may be a particular vulnerability to a sense of being too much for the counsellor, or of having done something wrong, which has precipitated the referral and their rejection by the counsellor. An example of this is where an onward referral may trigger resonances with a client's earlier experiences, or perceptions of being rejected when siblings were born after them. They may have a sense that the onward referral is made in order to move them along to make room for another client, who is imagined to have more entitlement to the therapist's time and energy, or as being more interesting to them. Also possible is that clients will experience a sense of themselves, or their feelings, as "too much" for the therapist, and therefore feel that they are being "sent away", potentially as a punishment for being too much trouble to them, or too needy emotionally. Again, this may resonate with a child or young person's early experience of being cared for by someone who indeed found their needs overwhelming and hard to manage. If a therapist perceives that such feelings are emerging in the therapy during the referring on process, it can be of great benefit if these can be spoken about in the room. Having such feelings made explicit in the therapy, and finding that they can be tolerated by their counsellor, can do much to help relieve a client's anxiety regarding their relationships, as well as enabling these issues to be worked through to some extent rather than carried into the relationship with the new professional or service, and then potentially acted-out. The referring on process can become potentially fertile ground for the working-through of important issues such as abandonment and rejection, while also offering an opportunity for the client to experience someone with whom they have formed an attachment being able to facilitate and survive their separation. This can be very important for adolescents who have not been given a sense by their parents that the family can survive their departure into adulthood and independence.

It is therefore important that the processing of any onward referral is given as much time and therapeutic space as possible and, in a similar approach to that of the termination of therapy, the emerging issues are not avoided or shied away from, but rather brought out and confronted appropriately.

Ending or "pausing" counselling

The previous case example demonstrated the process involved when an onward referral does not require the ongoing counselling to end, but simply to be modified while treatment takes place elsewhere. This will not always be the case, and with some clients it may be necessary for counselling to be terminated or to be "put on hold" while treatment takes place. The reasons why this might be the case are many. In practical terms, it may not be possible for families to fund different treatments concurrently if this is necessary, or even to logistically get their children to several different sessions during the week. For children and young people whose time is already over-committed, or who are managing academic pressures and/or the stress of exams, it may be too much for them to continue to attend counselling alongside other treatment.

If counselling is to come to an end in order for another treatment or therapeutic relationship to begin, as discussed previously, it is important that there is adequate space in counselling sessions for this to be discussed and for thought and feelings regarding this to be explored. Sometimes practitioners may find themselves experiencing surprise at how seemingly easily young clients make the transition between therapists, and while it is important to give space to considering issues around termination, it may not always be relevant for the client to dwell on these. Therefore discussions regarding transition should be client-led rather than come from an idea in the therapist that this is what the client *will* be feeling. Conversations may be necessary with the client and their family regarding a possible return to counselling in the future, and it can be helpful if practitioners are able to leave the "door open" for this possibility.

Other services for children and young people

As well as the GP and CAHMS services which counsellors working in private practice might refer to or consult with, there are other agencies working with children and families which counsellors may need to be aware of. The following outlines some of these in terms of their relationship with the therapist in private practice.

Local authority services

Chapter Five looked at the issue of law and confidentiality, and considered when a therapist might need to consider breaching confidentiality and making a referral to the police or local authority services for children and families if they considered a child might be at risk of significant harm. Referring on in these circumstances can often be particularly difficult for counsellors, as there can be a lack of clarity regarding the necessity of breaking confidentiality, especially in circumstances where there has not been consent with a resultant sense of loss of control for both client and practitioner if local authority services become involved.

In their book *Therapy with Children* (2010), Daniels and Jenkins make a strong case for counsellors to consider carefully the potential impact of a referral to the local authority when they consider the client or another to be at risk of significant harm. They are clear that for UK counsellors in private practice there is no mandatory reporting of child abuse, although there is a public interest defence for doing so, and that therefore counsellors working with young people outside of agency guidelines considering the reporting of abuse need to consider their actions carefully in this regard.

Where a therapist has made the decision based on their professional opinion derived from sound legal and ethical principles, and after consultation with their clinical supervisor, to approach the police or local authority children's services regarding their concerns, it is important to be prepared, to some extent, for the consequences.

As discussed in Chapter Five the HM Government guidelines, "What to do if you're worried a child is being abused" (2006), provides useful information for practitioners regarding when to make a referral to children's services or the police as well as outlining the procedures which will be followed after a referral has been made.

Impact on the therapeutic relationship

Just as previously discussed in the context of onward referrals due to mental health issues, a referral to social services will have an impact on the ongoing therapeutic relationship between client, therapist, and family, even when the referral is made with the client's consent and the family's knowledge and support. When the referral is made without the consent of the client, the impact can be significant and, on some occasions, the therapeutic relationship may not survive. When confidentiality is breached without consent, a client may feel that they no longer have trust in their therapy or their therapist. For this reason, it is essential that therapists making a referral to the authorities without a client's explicit consent are very clear in their own minds what their basis is for the breach, as well as having discussed it thoroughly in supervision beforehand.

The following case example shows how a therapist might come to make the decision to refer without consent, and what the implications for the therapeutic relationship might be.

Case example—Leila and Rita. Part One

Leila is a thirteen-year-old client being seen by Rita for weekly counselling sessions in her private counselling practice. Leila is originally referred by her dad due to her angry behaviour at home towards both him and herself. Rita learns at the assessment with Leila's dad that Leila's mum left the family home when Leila was nine years old and her sister, Kat, was seven. Initially mum went to live abroad with another man, and the girls had no contact with her at all for two years. At this time, both girls had some counselling via their primary school, which dad thinks they found helpful. In the last two years, mum has settled back in the UK, and the girls have had some contact with her. Recently this has included Leila spending the weekend occasionally with mum at her home with her new boyfriend and their eighteen-month-old daughter, Leila and Kat's half-sister. Dad confides to Rita at the assessment that he finds these weekends difficult as he still feels angry towards mum for abandoning the girls and him, but he recognises that they need to see their mum and sister, and knows that they are both keen to see her, but that Leila in particular wants to see her mum.

When Rita meets with Leila for an initial session she gets the impression that Leila very much idolises her mum, and is impressed by the wealthy lifestyle she has with her new partner. In their first few sessions following the assessment, Rita finds the work quite difficult and Leila hard to engage. Leila spends much of the session talking about her friends and all the ways in which they have disappointed her and let her down. She seems to avoid any attempts on Rita's part to engage her in talking about feelings or her behaviour at home. Rita begins to feel bored in the sessions and dreads Leila coming. Rita decides to discuss the work with Leila in supervision. In supervision, Rita and her supervisor reflect on the idea that Leila may be defending against forming an attachment with Rita which could leave her vulnerable to being catastrophically hurt and abandoned again, just as she was by her mum. Rita agrees that this could be the case, and can see that her feelings in the session could be understood as a countertransference response to Leila's emotional material. With this understanding Rita finds it easier to understand how to work with Leila, and they begin to form a tentative therapeutic alliance.

After the sixth session, Rita holds a review with Leila's dad over the phone. He says that he is beginning to notice a slight calming of Leila's mood generally except when she returns after spending the weekend with her mum. At these times he finds Leila angrier with him than ever. He wonders if it is because she feels sad to come home to him after being with her mum. He has also noticed that Leila has started to pull out her hair and eyelashes again, behaviour which she exhibited when her mum originally left, but which she has not done for some time. They agree that he will keep an eye on the development of this behaviour, but not do anything at the moment.

At her next session when they are talking about friends at school who have been giving Leila a hard time, she suddenly blurts out that she hates her mum's boyfriend and that he is a horrible man. When Rita asks her what she means, she is quiet and then says it was nothing. Leila says that she fears that if she tells Rita, Rita will tell her dad, and then she won't get to see her mum anymore. Rita is concerned by this, but decides not to put any pressure on Leila. She reminds her that they have agreed at the start of the work that Rita will keep everything Leila says in her counselling sessions confidential unless it seems that Leila is in danger of serious harm either from herself or from someone else. This is in order to make sure that Leila is kept safe, Rita assures her. Leila just carries on talking about her friends until the end of the session.

During their next session, Leila decides to talk about a friend whose mum has a boyfriend who has hurt her friend when she stayed with them. Leila tells Rita that her friend is very upset and feels quite frightened of him and isn't sure she wants to go and see her mum anymore. Rita says that she wonders if Leila is talking about her own situation, and Leila breaks down and says that she is. She tells Rita that her mum's boyfriend gets very angry and shouts "all the time" when he gets home from work in the city.

He has grabbed Leila around the top of her arm a few times and bruised her and has also pinned her against the wall and shouted in her face. Leila says that she has also seen him hit her mum, and that the baby was in her highchair when this happened. Leila is adamant that Rita mustn't tell anyone as she is terrified that her mum won't see her anymore if she finds out that Leila has "grassed" on her step-father.

Rita tells Leila that it was important that she told Rita about what is happening and that now they can take steps to keep Leila safe. She asks Leila for her permission to tell her dad what has been happening, before they decide what further action to take. Leila gets very upset and refuses to give Rita her permission. She says that she wishes she hadn't said anything and that she doesn't care what happens to her, but she can't lose her mum again. Rita repeats that she understands that Leila is very scared about losing touch with her mum, and that this must remind her of a very painful time in her childhood, but that the most important thing for now is to make sure that Leila and her little sister are both safe, and that the adults who care for them understand when their behaviour is damaging and unacceptable. As the end of the session is approaching, Rita asks Leila once more if she will consent to Rita talking to her dad. Leila refuses and Rita says that she will need to speak to him in that case without Leila's consent. At this point their time is up and Leila storms out of the room, slamming the door as she leaves.

Rita makes the decision to speak to Leila's dad that evening. She is concerned that Leila has left in a state of high anxiety regarding her disclosure and has some fears that this may lead to her self-harming. Rita contacts her supervisor beforehand and they discuss how Rita should respond in the situation. Rita's supervisor reminds her that as Leila is thirteen and considered Gillick competent she has the right to expect her disclosure to remain confidential, unless there is a risk that to do so would be to leave her at risk of significant harm. Her supervisor asks Rita if she is certain that the information that Leila disclosed is fact and not fantasy on Leila's part. Her supervisor asks Rita if she saw any bruising or evidence of physical abuse. Rita says that she did not, but that she is as certain as she can be that the events Leila described are fact. Rita's supervisor agrees that if Rita is as certain as possible that to keep Leila's disclosure confidential is not in either Leila's or the public interest, then she should consider breaking confidentiality, and speaking to Leila's dad, and the local authority children's services.

Rita contacts Leila's dad when she finishes seeing her clients that evening. He tells Rita that Leila has been shut in her room since returning from the session earlier. Rita tells him that she has made the decision to break confidentiality without Leila's consent as she is concerned that Leila and her sisters are potentially at risk of abuse from their mum's partner. She then tells him that she is going to contact the local social services and inform them of her concerns, and advises him that they will make contact with him as part of their investigation. Leila's dad is initially shocked by what Rita has told him, and then grateful to her for passing on the information. Rita says that it is possible that Leila will be very angry with Rita for disclosing the information, and may not want to come to her session next week. She suggests that Leila's dad does no more than gently encourage her to attend, and that, if she doesn't want to, she is not forced to come. They agree to keep in contact regarding any social services investigation as appropriate.

Following this conversation, Rita prepares a written report for social services detailing the disclosure which raised her concerns regarding Leila's safety. She includes details of Leila's name, address, and date of birth, as well as Leila's dad's name. Rita does not have any information regarding Leila's mother so this is not included. Rita includes in the report details of the conversation that she has had with Leila's dad, and also the fact that the report has been written without Leila's consent. The following morning Rita contacts the duty team at the local social services and lets them know that she will also drop in the written report later that day. The duty team let her know that they will now investigate the information she has given them and then let her know the outcome, or come back to her if they need any further information.

Rita then contacts her supervisor and lets her know the course of action she has taken. They agree to discuss this in more detail at the face-to-face session later in the week.

The case example above demonstrates circumstances where a counsellor might decide to break consent and refer a client and their family to social services or to the police if they suspect a serious crime has been committed. Rita follows her own professional protocol of offering clients a limited confidentiality from the start of the counselling, which is dependent upon them not being placed at risk if confidentiality is maintained. Her professional protocol also requires her to discuss the potential breach with her clinical supervisor before taking any action. In the event that their supervisor is unavailable, counsellors in private practice will need to contact another senior practitioner who they trust has the knowledge and experience to consider the matter with them.

Rita then follows the UK government advice for professionals on what to do if abuse is suspected and makes a referral accordingly.

The following return to the case example looks at the impact on the therapeutic relationship following on from the referral.

Case example—Leila and Rita. Part Two

Having made the referral to the local social services, Rita is left waiting to hear what will happen next. The following Tuesday, when she is due to meet with Leila for their session, she hears from Leila's dad to say that Leila is refusing to come to her session that afternoon. Leila's dad tells Rita that is has been a difficult week and that Leila has been very upset and angry. She is particularly angry with Rita who she feels very let down by. Rita is careful not to discuss this in too much detail with Leila's dad as she doesn't want to further damage the relationship with Leila in case she does return to therapy at some point. Leila's dad tells Rita that a social worker has been to see the girls, and that they are in the process of looking into any suspected abuse at Leila's mum's house. In the meantime, the girls are waiting to hear whether they can still meet with their mum that weekend, although they are not expecting to go to her house as their dad has already ruled that out himself.

Rita writes to Leila after the missed session letting her know that she missed her and that she hopes she will see her the following week when she will keep her space for her. Rita adds in the letter that she realises that Leila may be feeling upset and angry and that, even if she does not want to continue with her counselling with Rita, it might be helpful for her to come and talk about how she is feeling.

During the week Rita hears from social services who want to go over her report again. They have passed the matter on to colleagues in the area where Leila's mum lives, and they are investigating any issues to do with Leila's youngest sister. They will not be placing Leila on the child protection register and are advising that the girls spend time with their mum away from her home while the investigation is continuing.

The next week Rita hears from Leila's dad to say that Leila is still refusing to come to counselling and that the girls' mum is now saying she is not sure if she can continue to see them. Leila is very distressed and angry, and he has taken her back to the GP to see if they can get some further help from CAMHS. Rita reluctantly agrees with him that they may need to put Leila's counselling on hold for the time being. He says he hopes that at some point Leila will agree to see Rita again as he felt the sessions were beginning to help her.

When Rita goes to supervision that week she feels confused and angry regarding the outcome of her actions in terms of Leila not returning to therapy. Rita's supervisor encourages her to think through her actions and consider whether she would have done anything differently. They discuss together the difficulty of managing a situation where information arises in a counselling session which indicates that the client or another child or vulnerable adult is at risk. They consider that Rita has a protocol for dealing with child protection matters in her practice, and that she had contracted along the lines of this protocol with Leila when the counselling started.

Rita and her supervisor also discuss the outcome of Rita's actions. Rita is concerned that as Leila has not been able to return to therapy following the break of confidentiality it may not have been in her best interest, in spite of the protocol, to follow the child protection procedure. They discuss how this is an example of when keeping a child safe becomes the paramount consideration, potentially at the cost of the continuation of their therapy.

Rita's supervisor is careful to consider with Rita whether the outcome this time will affect how she responds should a similar situation arise in the future. Rita agrees that she will need to be mindful of this as she feels unhappy with how this has turned out.

This case example is intended to demonstrate the complexity for counsellors in private practice of referring on to social services in cases of suspected, or even known, abuse. Very often therapists, along with their clinical supervisors, are required to make difficult decisions where there are competing priorities to consider. As discussed in a previous chapter it is therefore important that counsellors support themselves in these matters by having a clear protocol of their own based on professional, ethical, and legal considerations for how they will act in these circumstances. Operating such a protocol does not, however, mean that outcomes can necessarily be controlled by either therapist or client, and therefore therapists must be prepared to work through any impact on the therapy or on themselves as therapists which occurs in these circumstances.

Further action and legal proceedings

It is certainly not the case that all referrals to the local authority will be without the consent of the client or their family, and there are other outcomes of a referral which therapists need to consider. If a client is being abused, or there has been historical abuse at some point in their life which is then investigated, there may be legal proceedings and potentially a court case following on from any investigation. Where legal proceedings are not indicated, the child and/or other children may be placed on a child protection register in order for continuing monitoring by social services to take place.

Counsellors can often experience anxiety regarding their position, and the position of the therapy when working with a child who is part of legal proceedings or a court case whether civil, for example in divorce and custody cases, or criminal. According to Jenkins (2005b); "The message frequently conveyed to therapists is that *any* therapy will be seen to contaminate and undermine the effectiveness of a child's evidence in court, and should, therefore, be delayed until after the conclusion of any proceedings" (Jenkins, 2005b, p. 87). This could potentially make it difficult for therapists to provide their client with the therapeutic support they are likely to very much need at that point, although as Jenkins (2005b) goes on to write;

> The position has been clarified by Practice Guidance, which clarifies that the Crown Prosecution Service does not, in fact, hold a veto over pre-trial therapy for child witnesses. Nevertheless an accommodation between the therapy and the needs of the law must be carefully negotiated and respected by all parties, if the needs of the child are to be properly met. (Jenkins, 2005b, p. 87)

Other onward referrals

As well as the main examples of onward referrals shown in the above, therapists can find themselves making onward referrals to other agencies during the course of therapy with children and young people. These might be into primary care services but due to issues of physical rather than mental health. Counsellors working with children may come to believe during the course of their counselling that they have an aspect of their physical health which requires further attention or investigation, and the counsellor will need to work with the client, and potentially their family with regards to this matter.

It may also be that issues arise relating to a client's learning abilities requiring an onward referral to speech and language specialists, or an educational psychologist. It may be that parents can manage this kind of onward referral through their child's school, but the service may require information from the counsellor regarding their concerns, and the usual care regarding confidentiality of client material is required here.

Some young clients have highly complex needs, and may require counselling alongside working with a number of different agencies offering support at different times. It is important for a counsellor working in such a circumstance to develop a protocol for information sharing which is realistic regarding the circumstances, but which has at its core a determination to meet the best interests of the client.

Summary

- There are circumstances where additional interventions may need to take place outside of the therapeutic work. This can be for a number of reasons.
- Counsellors and therapists must be aware of their own professional limitations and of the limitations of the therapy they are offering and work within these limits at all times.
- An onward referral must be made wherever possible with the knowledge and consent of the client and, where appropriate, their family.
- Therapists must be aware of the importance of maintaining their duty of confidentiality to their client's material while sharing information with other professionals.
- There may be circumstances where an onward referral needs to be made without the client's consent and the impact on the therapeutic relationship and on the client must be carefully monitored in these circumstances.
- Therapists should consult with their clinical supervisors regarding onward referrals and should use supervision sessions as an opportunity to reflect on the impact of a referral on the therapy both pre- and post such a referral taking place.

CHAPTER EIGHT

Training, supervision, and support networks

Throughout the previous chapters of this book I have emphasised the complexity and demands of working with children in private practice as well as the skills and knowledge required by the practitioner engaging in this work. It is important therefore that those preparing for practise in this area have established a solid foundation of training, clinical supervision, and support which is then maintained on an ongoing basis. In the following we explore how practitioners might go about this in a way that is appropriate and meets the needs of their individual practice. To begin, the chapter takes a brief look at the development of professional standards across the profession as a whole in order to gain a sense of the fundamental requirements for practitioners.

Professional standards in counselling and psychotherapy

The field of counselling and psychotherapy has become increasingly concerned in recent years with the importance of ensuring that those working in the profession are adequately trained and supported, in order to enable them to provide the best possible therapy to their clients and patients. In the UK, unlike in the USA and elsewhere, there is no official government regulation of those choosing to describe themselves as counsellors and psychotherapists. This has understandably given rise to concerns amongst professionals and the public alike regarding who is presenting themselves as a counsellor or psychotherapist and what their training and skill level is. Clients entering therapy can often be at particularly vulnerable points in their lives and it is important that they are able to have some assurance, when they approach someone offering therapy, that the professional they are seeing is trained and supervised properly. This is arguably of even greater importance in the field of counselling children and young people due to the particular vulnerabilities of this group. As a result, in recent years the therapy profession in the UK and elsewhere has increasingly become self-regulating, leading to the establishment of national registers for therapy practitioners.

The counselling and psychotherapy industry has grown enormously in recent years in terms of the numbers of therapists in practice and people seeking therapy, whether for themselves, their relationship, their children or an organisation (BACP, 2014b). Increasingly people seem aware of the potential benefits of therapy in helping them to address difficulties they may encounter in their lives and, alongside this increase in demand, more individuals are deciding to train as therapists, and correspondingly more institutions are providing a range of training for the field.

Many of those in the UK seeking a counsellor or psychotherapist may now be aware of the various bodies representing the profession such as the BACP (British Association for Counselling and Psychotherapy), UKCP (UK Council for Psychotherapy), and COSCA (Counselling and Psychotherapy in Scotland). These organisations all hold registers of their members and expect them to have reached a certain standard of training as a practitioner as well as agreeing to adhere to a code of ethics before advertising or describing themselves as a counsellor or psychotherapist. These organisations also accredit and regulate therapy trainings in the UK along with offering further accreditations to practitioners who have reached high standards of training and experience in their particular field.

As the interest in the training and skills in the profession has increased in general, there has been a corresponding interest in the training and skills of those practitioners working therapeutically with children and young people. The BACP offers a separate membership division for those working children and young people and the UKCP have recently begun to hold a separate register of psychotherapists who have completed a training in child and adolescent therapy and are practising with this group. The BACP also offers those who have completed an initial counsellor/psychotherapist accreditation the opportunity to apply for the title of senior accredited counsellor/psychotherapist of children and young people with an emphasis on the practitioner having completed further training and supervised practice hours in the field. These registers and accreditations offer the public assurance when seeking a professional to work with their child or family that the practitioner is trained and experienced in work with children and young people.

Training in work with children and young people

The next section of this chapter will look at the different types of training available for practitioners wishing to work in this field, and offers some assistance in thinking about what level of training may be most suitable for individual therapists.

Practitioners may come to this book from differing backgrounds as far as previous training in the field is concerned and therapists come from many different routes to working therapeutically with children and young people in private practice or in other settings. Reflecting this are a range of trainings which offer the potential to fulfil various training needs and prepare therapists to work at a variety of levels of intensity with children and young people, in a variety of modalities and methods.

In the UK, arguably the most intensive level of training in therapeutic work with children and adolescents is as a child and adolescent psychoanalytic psychotherapist. The Association of Child Psychotherapists (ACP) sets out a high standard of training requirements for those wishing to become members of their organisation. Trainees are expected to complete a four year doctorate programme including elements such as clinical placements in a variety of NHS and CAMHS settings, academic study, and high-frequency personal therapy throughout. This training would prepare practitioners for working with a variety of ages at a high intensity in a range of settings.

There are alternative institutions in the UK who currently offer stand-alone trainings in child psychotherapy and counselling at a lower intensity than the ACP training requires. These may be accredited by the BACP or lead to registration as a child psychotherapist with the UKCP. Some trainings are offered or validated by universities around the UK and consist of Post graduate diplomas or Masters' courses which offer the opportunity to train with children and adolescents in a variety of settings. These trainings are offered by a variety of institutions and organisations with an emphasis on different modalities or methods of working with this group. They will generally all cover modules on; child development, attachment theory, family dynamics, safeguarding children at risk, training in the delivery of therapy to children and young people in various modalities and, increasingly, the relevance of neuroscience in emotional development. Some trainings, particularly those in child psychotherapy, will also include a mother and infant observation and a psychiatric placement. For the clinical component of the training, trainees will be expected to complete a placement working therapeutically with children of the relevant age group and at the required intensity. This will clearly vary according to the type of training undertaken. Most trainings require participants to undertake their own personal therapy for at least some part of the duration of the course.

More details of how to find out which courses are currently available and where are included in the useful resources section at the end of the book.

A stand-alone training such as those outlined above in therapeutic work with children and adolescents will prepare trainees thoroughly in various aspects of work with this group but will not usually qualify them to also work with adult clients.

Conversion courses or "add-on" trainings

For counsellors and psychotherapists already qualified in therapeutic work with adults there are various options for training should they wish to extend their practice to include children and/or adolescents.

Many of the colleges and institutions who offer trainings in child psychotherapy and counselling also provide courses allowing suitably qualified practitioners to convert their initial training with adults into one preparing them for work with children. These conversion courses will generally include elements covering the theories of child development, practical and professional issues in work with children, a mother and infant observation, personal therapy, and a supervised clinical placement. Prospective trainees will need to check the requirements of individual organisations to ensure their initial training is of the required standard to be accepted for the conversion. These trainings are often accredited by a relevant professional body and will lead to registration as a child psychotherapist or counsellor.

For those practitioners not able or wishing to complete a full conversion training but preferring to build their own portfolio of training, tailored to the individual needs of their practice and completed at their own pace, there are many organisations offering shorter, postqualifying courses in all aspects of therapeutic work with children and young people. These will include training and CPD (continuing professional development) workshops covering both the fundamentals as well as other aspects of therapeutic work with this group. Often the organisations offering these training opportunities advertise details of these courses on their websites, via twitter and Facebook or through the publications of the relevant professional bodies. By completing a variety of these courses and workshops, qualified practitioners can build their own portfolio of training in therapeutic work with children and young people in a way which is relevant to the requirements of their own practice.

BACP Senior Accredited Counsellor of Children and Young People

The BACP currently offers practitioners who are already qualified and accredited by them the option to apply for the status of Senior Accredited Counsellor/Psychotherapist of children and young people. Application is open to those who have held BACP accredited status for at least three years and who meet the criteria shown in the table below:

Table 9.1. Criteria for BACP Senior Accreditation as Counsellor/ Psychotherapist Children and Young People.

BACP Senior Accredited Counsellor of children and young people

To meet the criteria for senior accreditation, practitioners must be:

1. An accredited counsellor/psychotherapist member of BACP and thereby comply with the association's *Ethical Framework for Good Practice in Counselling and Psychotherapy.*
2. Covered by professional indemnity insurance.
3. Be in current practice as a counsellor/psychotherapist for children and young people.
4. Have an ongoing contract for counselling/psychotherapy supervision for a minimum of one and a half hours per month for each month in which practice is undertaken with a supervisor who is experienced in working therapeutically with children and/or young people.
5. Have undertaken a minimum of 300 hours of supervised counsellor/ psychotherapist practice over at least three years since initial accreditation, *of which a minimum of 100 hours are with children and/or young people.*
6. Have a minimum of ninety hours of CYP related CPD relevant to your role as a counsellor/psychotherapist over at least three years since initial accreditation. This must contain child and adolescent development and legal, safeguarding and ethical issues.

These criteria are correct as of January 2015 but may be subject to change.

Practitioners who meet the above criteria are then required to complete case studies demonstrating various aspects of their understanding of the work and their practice. This allows appropriately qualified and accredited practitioners to receive recognition of their achievement of a portfolio of training and supervised practice in the field of counselling children and young people.

Continuing professional development (CPD)

It is a requirement for all practitioners who are members of a professional body to engage in CPD activities in order to develop their practice and keep it up to date. CPD is an excellent way of exploring new areas of work which are of interest without committing to a full training, and also helps practitioners identify and explore areas of practice where they feel they could benefit from more support or information.

Attending CPD events such as workshops or conferences offers the opportunity to meet up with others working in the same or similar fields. The kind of courses or workshops mentioned above would be of use to practitioners looking for CPD as well as those looking to train in work with children and young people. It can be very useful for practitioners to use their clinical supervision to consider alongside their supervisor what might be an appropriate path for them to take regarding CPD, particularly if they are considering applying for accreditation with a particular professional body.

An important recent development in counselling CPD in the UK has been the counselling MindEd programme developed by the BACP, funded by the Department of Health. Counselling MindEd is part of the MindEd project which makes online learning available to all those working with children and young people. Counselling MindEd is specifically geared towards trainee and qualified counselling practitioners wishing to develop their knowledge in various aspects of therapeutic work with children and young people using e-learning modules. It is not considered as a replacement for the need for face-to-face training or CPD for practitioners and trainees, but as an additional resource for their use. Practitioners can complete modules whenever they wish in order to best supplement their practice. Details of how to access MindEd can be found in the useful resources section of this book.

Clinical supervision

Throughout this book emphasis has been placed on the importance of clinical supervision for the therapist working with children and young people in private practice. Regular clinical supervision is central to the practice of all therapists whether trainees or qualified and experienced. It serves a number of purposes including; the provision of a learning environment, a reflective space to consider unconscious aspects of the work, somewhere to consider ethical issues, a place for practitioners to go to for professional support at difficult times as well as a space for reflecting on any professional needs and areas for professional development. The professional bodies in the UK all stress in their ethical frameworks the need for therapists to make arrangements for ongoing clinical supervision. The BACP states in its *Ethical Framework* that;

7. All counsellors, psychotherapists, trainers and supervisors are required to have regular and on-going formal supervision/consultative support for their work in accordance with professional requirements. (BACP, 2013, p. 5)

While the UKCP uses its statement on supervision as an opportunity to emphasise the importance of it's use as an aid to helping when practitioners face complex decisions regarding referring clients on, as discussed in an earlier chapter of this book;

5.7 The psychotherapist accepts responsibility to ensure that they are competent and have sufficient supervisory arrangements and other necessary support to enable them to meet their psychotherapeutic obligations to any client. This includes the responsibility of ensuring the very careful consideration of how best to refer a client to another psychotherapist or professional should it become clear that this would be in the client's best interest. (UKCP, 2009, p. 6)

These statements make clear that the supervisory relationship provides an important foundation for all clinical work undertaken by practitioners. Clearly supervision will fulfil different functions at different points in the practitioner's work life and therefore it is important that supervision provision is found which can be flexible enough to support various aspects of their practice as it develops and changes.

There is some potential for therapists working with children and young people in private practice to feel isolated and possibly overwhelmed at times, especially if they have not managed to create adequate support structures for themselves. As this book attempts to demonstrate, this is a complex area for therapists to work in and one which can, at times, present a practitioner with some complex issues to manage without the relative safety of organisational or statutory guidelines and policies to support them. In this respect, clinical supervision has particular importance for the practitioner in private practice and therefore it is important that care is taken when they go about considering what their supervisory needs are and how best to meet them.

Difference of setting

One of the main issues which this book has tried to emphasise is that of the difference between working with children in private practice and working with the same group in another setting. It is no doubt the case that much of the knowledge and practical skill required in engaging and working with children therapeutically is transferable across settings, but by no means all. A clinical supervisor who has a great deal of experience in working therapeutically with children and adolescents in a school or CAMHS setting may have much to offer their supervisees in terms of their knowledge of child and adolescent development, and their experience in therapeutic work, but they may not have as much or any experience in supporting a practitioner with those issues which are specific to work with children and young people in the private practice setting. If a practitioner is thinking of extending their private practice to include children and young people it may be useful for them to seek supervision with someone who has experience and understanding of the complex issues involved in this undertaking. If a supervisor already has prior awareness of what the issues may be with working in this setting, it can be hoped that it will not be necessary for the supervisee to explain these aspects of the work to their supervisor, in order that the client material be understood in context. It is also important that supervisors have up to date knowledge of the law as it relates to therapy with children in private practice in order that they are able to work alongside their supervisee in considering any ethical and/or legal dilemmas they may be facing.

Peer supervision

While many practitioners consider a one-to-one supervisory relationship with their clinical supervisor to be the most beneficial in terms of meeting their needs of supervision, they may also look to other ways of receiving supervisory support, either as an alternative to one-to-one sessions or in addition. It is for individual therapists to ensure that their supervision meets the needs of their practice as well as fulfils the requirements of their professional body. This will assist in enabling them to provide good quality and ethically sound therapy to their clients and patients. Some therapists may prefer to receive at least some of their supervision in a one-to-one setting, preferably with a supervisor whose own skills and experience can meet the needs of the supervisee's practice. An alternative, which it may be useful to consider for therapists working with children in private practice, possibly in addition to their core one-to-one supervision, is peer supervision. Peer supervision can be understood as a group of therapists coming together for the purpose of offering each other clinical supervision of their practice. The members can be formed from those who work in a similar setting and thus have an understanding of the kind of work being undertaken, but also may come from different modalities or have different approaches to the work. In this respect the peer group can offer both a secure foundation of understanding of the context in which members are working, along with the capacity to reflect on the clinical work presented by "supervisees" from different perspectives. There are clearly disadvantages as well as advantages to supervision delivered in a peer setting. Becoming part of a peer supervision group offers therapists the opportunity to think with other colleagues about their work, therefore limiting any sense of isolation the private practitioner may be experiencing in their practice. It can be useful to have a broader knowledge base to draw from and a group can provide different pieces of useful information and ideas regarding the work which individuals may find beneficial. However, there can be pitfalls to working in groups and in particular in working in leaderless groups as represented by the peer supervision group. In *Supervision in the Helping Professions*, Hawkins and Shoet (2012) discuss the benefits of this kind of supervision but also emphasise the importance of clear boundaries when the group is formed as well as the importance of members being aware of the kind of issues which can become played out and potentially be harder to address when there is not a designated facilitator or leader of the group; "Peer groups also need to have a system for attending to their own process so that it stays healthily supportive of the task of supervision rather that diverting or sabotaging it" (Hawkins & Shoet, 2012, p. 195).

However practitioners decide to arrange their supervision it is important that they do so with care and with consideration of the needs of their practice. This may also require reviewing from time to time to ensure that they and therefore their client are adequately supported.

Additional support networks

As previously stated, practising as a therapist can be a somewhat isolating profession and this may particularly be so in private practice. In other settings such as education or CAMHS, practitioners may find themselves working as part of a team, and while this can at times present its own challenges, there is an element of support for the individual working in this way which is largely absent from the day-to-day work life of the private practitioner. In this respect, private practitioners who run their practice from home need to be particularly careful in ensuring that their needs to interact with and be supported by other colleagues are not neglected or minimised.

Therapists working with children and young people have a lot to think about in their work, as this book has hopefully set out. They must negotiate relationships with parents and other family members, some-times when those families are going through separations and other complications; they need to keep abreast of current law as it relates to child welfare and safeguarding while also considering complex issues such as Gillick competency and informed consent; they encounter work involving risk of harm and need to be able to help young people negoti-ate their development into the adult world and their need to separate and individuate; and they must do all of this while also keeping an eye on the therapeutic impact of rapid advances in digital technology! While supervision is a vital tool in providing practitioners with support in negotiating all these areas and more, it can also be very helpful for practitioners working therapeutically with children in private practice to be aware that they are not alone in doing so and to hear about ways in which others are managing some of the issues and aspects of the work outlined above. It can therefore be highly beneficial for practition-ers working in this context to take advantage of any opportunities for networking with others in a similar position and to develop their own support networks with colleagues.

As discussed earlier, one of the ways to do this can be to take part in CPD opportunities. Many of the professional bodies and training organisations run workshops and conferences where there are plenty of opportunities to meet colleagues and share a diversity of knowledge and experience, as well as to explore new ideas regarding best practice. Taking a course or attending a workshop should not only be seen as a way of gaining new knowledge, but also of sharing practice and being supported by colleagues. Even if those we meet are not local and we may not even stay in touch, it can be enormously beneficial just to know that there are others out there all attempting to provide high quality therapy to children and families via their private practice.

Some of the professional bodies also provide the opportunity for therapists to take part in online forums with other therapy colleagues and this can be as useful way of making contact with those working in a similar field. There are also therapists who advertise local networking opportunities in the professional journals and if there isn't one in a particular locality then it may be possible for practitioners to start up their own.

As touched upon in an earlier chapter, it can also be beneficial for practitioners in private practice to develop a network of professional contacts to support their practice. This might consist of professionals such as a child and adolescent psychiatrist, an educational psychologist, local youth services, amongst many others. The exact composition of a professional network will depend on the locality individuals are working on and on who they come into contact with during the course of their work. This is another way in which peer supervision can be helpful, allowing as it does for the sharing of professional contacts as appropriate.

Therapists must ensure for the sake of themselves and their clients that they have the right support in terms of training and supervision in order to establish and develop a practice which will provide the best quality therapeutic support to their clients and families. This requires an ongoing commitment on the part of the individual practitioner to understanding their own needs in this respect and ensuring that they are adequately met.

Summary

- Practitioners working with children in private practice will require a solid foundation of training, supervision, and support in order to work effectively and ethically.
- The professional bodies have clear requirements of their members in respect of training and supervision which practitioners must be aware of and adhere to.
- Practitioners should reflect on their training needs on a regular basis and ensure that they are not practising beyond the scope of their skills and knowledge. CPD should be utilised to keep up-to-date.
- Clinical supervision is a vital component of practice and practitioners should ensure that their supervision provision is appropriate for the needs of their individual practice.
- Support networks of colleagues and professionals from other fields are vital for practitioners in private practice to maintain a sense of being connected to their profession and able to draw on the skills and knowledge of others when necessary.

PART IV

WORKING WITH TECHNOLOGY IN PRIVATE PRACTICE WITH CHILDREN AND YOUNG PEOPLE

CHAPTER NINE

The impact of digital technology and communication

The scope of this chapter is wide, covering different aspects of the relationship that counselling children and young people has with digital technology and communication. Issues relating to clients' experiences with cyberspace, social networking, and other modes of digital technology, frequently emerge in their counselling sessions. In an earlier chapter on working with risk, one aspect of online behaviour which has been seen in counselling sessions, that of "sexting", was explored along with a general overview of the risk young people may experience online. It is apparent just from this example that practitioners who are working with this group require some acquaintance with the "cyber" world which many young people now regularly inhabit.

There has been much written on the subject of how, whether, and why psychological therapies should be interested in and/or adopt cyberspace and digital technologies into their theoretical bases and practice. These range from ideas of economy and expediency regarding offering therapy online (Hollinghurst et al., 2010), discussions of the place of psychoanalytic thinking within computer culture and social networking (Balick, 2014; Turkle, 2004), and of the place of computers and digital technology in therapy (Brottman, 2012; Israeli, Asulin-Simhon & Sharabany, 2013). These ideas may be of particular relevance to practitioners working with children and young people as children are now arguably growing up in the "digital age", meaning that their social and emotional development could be viewed as inextricably connected with the Internet and online technology. Mindful of this, in 2001, teacher and writer Marc Prensky coined the terms "Digital Natives" and "Digital Immigrants" when he published a paper of the same name (Prensky, 2001). This paper outlined what he saw as the difference between those who have grown up and lived their whole lives in the digital age, and those who have come to it as adults, their thinking and processing already formed in an earlier culture. Prensky suggests that this generation may have different needs in terms of teaching and education, but his ideas could equally be applied to working therapeutically with this, and subsequent generations. Therapists working with young people now need to consider how being a "digital native" may have impacted on their client's development.

Prensky's ideas regarding learning and brain development in "digital natives", though widely disseminated, have received some criticism (Helsper & Enyon, 2010; Thompson, 2013). Some critics have taken issue with his use of neuroscience to qualify ideas regarding the brain development of those who grow up in the digital age, and the ways in which this makes them fundamentally different to older generations, however thoroughly they may have adopted and adapted to developments and advances in technology. Helsper and Enyon (2010) offer an alternative perspective in their paper in response to Prensky (2001) where they discuss the results of their research into whether there really is such a chasm between "digital natives" and "digital immigrants" as Prensky (2001) imagines.

Whether or not growing up in the digital age fundamentally alters the thinking of "digital natives", it is likely to have had an impact on the way young people think of themselves and on the way they form relationships, both important factors in therapy with this group.

In *Born Digital: Understanding the First Generation of Digital Natives*, Palfrey and Gasser (2008) invite their readers to consider these impacts on those born post-1980, in the "digital age";

> We see promise in the way that Digital Natives are interacting with digital information, expressing themselves in social environments, creating new art forms, dreaming up new business models, and starting new activist ventures. The purpose of this book is to

separate what we need to worry about from what's not so scary,
what we ought to resist from what we ought to embrace. (Palfrey &
Gasser, 2008, p. 9)

This is also the spirit in which this chapter hopes to explore this area,
in terms of sustaining a curiosity in the particular meaning that digital technology has on the lives of our clients, from the particular perspective of the practitioner working therapeutically with children and
young people.

Technology and modern childhood

Over forty years ago, Erik Erikson (1971) wrote that; "The youth of
today is not the youth of twenty years ago. This much any elderly person would say, at any point in history, and think it was both new and
true" (Erikson, 1968, p. 26). In some respects, society is always "playing
catch-up" with the youth of the day, generally more familiar with new
technologies and advances as they naturally push against what is established and seen as belonging to their parents and the previous age. It
is, however, clear that recent advances in technology and, in particular,
digital technology have profoundly altered many aspects of daily life,
with perhaps the greatest impact being felt by those who are children
and adolescents in modern Western culture.

Children and adolescents in the West arguably develop and move
towards adulthood and independence in a world very different to that
of previous generations. Many of them live and develop socially not
only in the "real" world of home, school, and friendships, but also in
another digital world online, in "cyberspace". Israeli, Asulin-Simhon,
and Sharabany (2013) look at the implications of this world for young
people and for their therapy. They ask a question which is relevant to all
those engaged with this group: "Does cyberspace open up new chan-
nels through which the adolescent may grow and deal with developmental burdens, or does it merely further complicate his life?" (Israeli,
Asulin-Simhon, & Sharabany, 2013, p. 282). Therapists who work with
children and young people need to cultivate a sense of curiosity regarding what it is like to be growing up in whatever age and environment,
technological or otherwise, that they find themselves in.

There is a need to be acquainted with both the benefits and pitfalls of life in the digital age if practitioners are to continue to provide

the potential for a therapeutic engagement which is meaningful and appropriate for children and young people in the twenty-first century. It can be argued that some aspects of cyberspace and social networking are enormously beneficial to young people, some of whom may struggle, for a variety of reasons, with connections and relationships in the "real" or physical worlds of home and school. Much has been written regarding the capacity to create alternative identities online and therefore for young people to free themselves from aspects of their "real" selves which they feel might be undesirable to others, or which adversely affect their confidence. For example, a paper by Israeli, Asulin-Simhon, and Sharabany (2013) suggests that cyberspace may provide a sense of belonging for those who feel excluded and can act as, "a rehearsal space for social communication" (Israeli, Asulin-Simhon & Sharabany, 2013, p. 282). This envisages cyberspace as an experimental space for young people to "play" at social engagement without it affecting their "real" life. In this respect, cyberspace represents an online "playground" where young people are able to experiment safely with different identities, form relationships with their peers, and make attempts to discover who they are as well as who they would perhaps like to be. This idea can be expanded to take into account the Eriksonian idea of the adolescent moratorium, as Turkle (2004) does in the following;

> It is a time during which one's actions are, in a certain sense, not counted as they will be later in life. They are not given as much weight, not given the force of full judgment. In this context, experimentation can become the norm rather than a brave departure. Relatively consequence-free experimentation facilitates the development of a "core self," a personal sense of what gives life meaning that Erikson called "identity". (Turkle, 2004, p. 22)

Turkle (2004) goes on to envisage the modern online "virtual community" as a space where this experimentation and development can take place for contemporary adolescents, where once college would have fulfilled the requirement for such a moratorium in young peoples' lives.

We might think then of cyberspace as a kind of online sand tray for young peoples' experimentation and play. This is a concept which could be of great use to therapists working with children and young people. Just as they might observe a child playing with figures in the sand tray, a therapist can observe and listen in a similar way to a client talking about their online behaviour. They might notice how the client presents themselves in cyberspace, looking out for details of online behaviour such as; the creation of avatars (online characters often used in gaming or in virtual worlds) which could represent longed-for aspects of themselves, or parts that they don't feel they can safely express anywhere else (Dunn & Guadagno, 2012; Turkle, 2011); "blogging", whether clients are anonymous bloggers, hiding behind the disguise of a user name or use this as a means of direct self-expression and communication with an online "community"; a preoccupation with the image they project via the internet, expressed through the use of "selfies", and/or with how their numerous "friends" view them online. There is a world of useful material to be found by the therapist who is open to listening to a client's adventures in cyberspace, if the client is open to sharing them and is encouraged to do so. In order to facilitate this, it is important that therapists who are perhaps not so familiar with the digital world are not defensive or uninterested when clients want to bring it in and explore it in therapy. There is a balance to be sought between the demand for a practitioner to become an "expert" in an unfamiliar field and the rather "techno-phobic" attitude adopted by some, for whom the digital world seems too alien and confounding, and perhaps a little frightening at times.

Children, adolescents, and cyberspace

There is much research to suggest that children and young people spend an increasing amount of their time engaged in some way with digital technology (Mesch, 2012), particularly in recent years with the internet via mobile phone technology. Mesch (2012) argues that this increase in interaction with digital technology has had a major impact on the lives of young people, particularly in terms of social networks and in; "the acceleration of the process of autonomy from parents" (Mesch, 2012, p. 97). Turkle (2011) suggests that the impact of digital technology on young peoples' development is more complex than this suggests and highlights some of the paradoxes inherent in growing up in this technological age, particularly in respect of separation; "The network facilitates separation (a cell phone allows children greater freedom) but also inhibits it (a parent is always on tap)" (Turkle, 2011, p. 169).

It may be that practitioners see evidence of this in their therapeutic work with young people. For example, it can be difficult for a teenager to separate from an anxious parent and gain a sense of autonomy when the parent, for example, insists on tracking their child's movements using a mobile phone "app" to view their location. Equally, an anxious child may create a situation where they have constant access to their parent, even when away from home, therefore limiting situations where they will have to tolerate their parent's absence. Turkle (2011) uses the idea of modern young people being "tethered" by technology, to describe the impact of mobile phones on the process of gaining autonomy and separation from parents. For her, mobile phones can mean that young people growing up now may miss out on important opportunities to experience themselves as self-reliant. In her view they always have a parent or community of friends on the end of the phone to fall back on when necessary.

Turkle (2011) also expands this idea of being "tethered" into the realms of children's peer relationships, where she argues that there is a demand on them to be constantly available to peers and support their ongoing sense of existence. Practitioners may discover in their work that this kind of constant connectivity can greatly complicate the lives of their clients. Young people may struggle with the demand to be connected at all times and the pressure that this can bring with it. This constant connectivity may mean, for example, that bullying is extended out of the realms of "real" life situations such as school, and into the world of social networks, potentially creating a situation of no respite for the victim.

What this demonstrates is that alongside the increased opportunities for social connections, and potential improvements in self-esteem and wellbeing (Steinfeld, Ellison, & Lampe, 2008; Valkenburg & Peter 2007) which the internet arguably offers young people, it also brings the risk of increasing their vulnerability to negative social influences, such as cyber bullying and sexual exploitation, and it is often the most vulnerable young people who are likely to experience the more socially negative aspects of the internet. Steinberger (2009) suggests that the internet can provide instant gratification for those struggling to feel accepted and that can create a vulnerability in some; "For susceptible teens with impaired judgement, the instantaneous, private Internet connection is seductive, responding to instinctual wishes for sexual prowess, self-worth and narcissistic grandiosity" (Steinberger, 2009, p. 134). Many of the young people seen for counselling and psychotherapy will be vulnerable in the ways outlined in the above and therefore their online engagements may cause them considerable problems and require support from their therapy. It is increasingly important for therapists to have an understanding of the relationship that young people have with technology and the impact this might have upon their mental and emotional wellbeing.

It may be important also to share some of this understanding, where appropriate, with parents, who can be confused and frustrated by their child's relationship with technology and their attachments to their phones, tablets, and laptops. Parents can often decide to withdraw access to mobile phones, tablets or computers, having recognised their fundamental importance in their child's life, as a way of either punishing, coercing, or as an attempt to protect their children from the perceived dangers inherent in the internet. This removal of access to technology, whether carried out or merely threatened, can have an enormous impact on the child's anxiety levels, as well as place considerable strain on the relationship between parent and child. In such situations, practitioners may be able to offer assistance for parents in understanding their child's relationship with their technological devices, as well as in helping them to make choices and set boundaries which are appropriate and beneficial for their child, rather than pursuing those which contribute and/or exacerbate the problem.

The following case example looks at the way in which a client's engagement with cyberspace can provide useful material for the therapy:

Case example—Jane and Aidan

Aidan is a twelve-year-old boy who has been seeing Jane for weekly counselling sessions for two months, in her private practice. Aidan has been feeling anxious and unhappy since his parents separated acrimoniously six months previously, following the discovery of his father's long term affair with another woman. Aidan's mother is also seeing a counsellor due to her own acute anxiety following the separation which affects her badly at times. Aidan's father is now living with the woman with whom he had an affair, and Aidan has been refusing to see him.

During one of their sessions, Aidan asks Jane if she is on Facebook. Jane wonders with Aidan why he is asking, and he says that he has recently opened an account and wondered if she would be his friend as he doesn't have very many at the moment. Jane is aware that Aidan has been struggling with friendships, having also changed schools in the same month as his father left the family home, but she thinks there may be more to his request than this and begins to consider how best to work with it.

Jane considers the need to maintain the boundary around the therapeutic relationship in a way which feels safe for Aidan, but which does not add to his current feelings of anxiety regarding his capacity to make and maintain friends. Jane is also curious about what Aidan imagines it would be like to have her as a "Facebook friend" and she wonders if their therapeutic relationship is well enough established at this point to allow them to think about this together.

Jane initially reminds Aidan about the boundaries they discussed when they first met regarding their relationship and how they would only have contact with each other in their sessions in order that this would feel like a safe space for Aidan to use to share and explore his feelings. Jane says that she does know some things about Facebook but wonders if Aidan would tell her about how he is finding it on there.

Aidan begins to talk about how he feels bad about lying about his age to set up his profile but says that everyone in his class has Facebook already so he didn't want to be left out. He says that he has been trying to get as many friends as he can very quickly, but that everyone else seems to have more than him.

Jane is struck by his words that everyone "has more than him". When she asks about this, Aidan says that he is not just talking about friends, but about family too. He tells Jane that everyone he sees on Facebook has both their parents, and brothers and sisters, and other family members they are connected to. Jane realises that an action which he hoped would allow him to feel more connected to his peers and part of their group, has actually exposed Aidan to painful feelings of grief regarding the situation with his family.

Aidan talks about having seen one of his classmates posting photos of his new baby sister with his parents on Facebook. Aidan says that seeing this made him feel angry with his father and very sad too. Jane wonders if Aidan himself would have liked a baby brother or sister and is experiencing some sadness regarding this.

At this point Jane begins to wonder if Aidan's request to have her be his "friend" on Facebook may have been a way of trying to have her alongside him while he encountered some of this painful material in cyberspace. With this in mind, she begins to talk about how hard it must be for him to be seeing this material on Facebook, while he is going through such a difficult time in his own family, and wonders whether he feels quite alone with his feelings online. Aidan agrees that he does and they begin to talk more about this together.

Towards the end of the session Jane acknowledges to Aidan that it might be very disappointing for him that Jane is not his "friend" on Facebook and that she is not there to help him when he encounters things which make him feel sad or angry when he is online. Aidan says that he is pleased to have been able to talk about this with her in the session and feels that he might not feel so overwhelmed by what he sees on Facebook now.

When he returns for his session the following week, Aidan wants to talk again about his experiences on Facebook, telling Jane he has now made "friends" with a girl whose parents are divorced and who is an only child, and he doesn't feel as much as if he is the only one in this situation anymore.

This case example attempts to demonstrate how beneficial it can be for practitioners to be open exploring their client's material around cyberspace in the same way that they would approach all material in the session.

Most important, at a time when there is much interest from academia and the media in general about digital technology and social networks, is for therapists to not make assumptions about internet use in their clients, but rather to help them understand on an individual basis their relationships with cyberspace, and support them in managing them in a way which is beneficial and aids their development, as well as noticing where it might complicate or inhibits it.

Online therapy

There has been much written in recent years regarding offering therapy online and although it is beyond the scope of this book to explore the specifics of that rapidly developing branch of the profession in much detail, there are some aspects which are useful to examine here.

Online therapy, whether delivered via the writing and exchange of emails or "face-to-face" via software applications such as "Skype" and "FaceTime", is becoming a more viable and requested method of delivering therapy, in both agency settings and in private practice, and may be of relevance to those working with children and young people. The BACP are clear in their most recent set of published guidelines for online counsellors and psychotherapists that; "Online provision is a specialist area, requiring a level of competence at least as high as that for face-to-face work" (BACP, 2014a). This makes it clear that the BACP expects qualified therapists to seek further training in working online, before offering such a service to their clients.

The benefits of being able to work over the internet are many. Offering therapy online allows it to be accessible to clients who would otherwise be unable to attend due to illness, disability or remote locations. Clients who relocate to other areas of the country or globe would be able to continue their therapeutic relationship at a time when major upheavals in other areas of their life would mean this was highly beneficial for them, and clients residing outside of major cities could potentially be able to find a specialist working online who they may not have been able to work with if the internet were not available. The opportunity to work online also opens the profession up as a possibility for those without regular access to a consultation room or who are disabled or remotely located themselves.

Online therapy for children and young people

Working online can be argued to be of particular relevance with children and young people given what has already been said regarding their familiarity with, and perhaps even preference for, online digital means of communication. For some therapists, the leap from a face-to-face therapeutic relationship where client and practitioner are both physically present in the same location synchronously, to therapy which takes place over an internet connection and between people who may be very far apart geographically, can feel too great. Some practitioners may have concerns that it will not be possible to establish a therapeutic alliance over the internet, or that they will not be able to continue to work with transference and countertransference phenomena.

There are clearly differences to be considered between the various kinds of online therapeutic interventions available. Seeing a client for regular sessions via video-hosting applications such as "FaceTime" or "Skype" for example, is a very different undertaking to therapy in written form over email or text. There are further differences in offering email or text where practitioner and client are communicating synchronously and those interventions which take place over extended periods of time. There has been, and continues to be, much interest and research into these areas in recent years (Amichai-Hamburger et al., 2014; Goss & Anthony, 2009) some of which looks in particular at these issues as they relate specifically to therapy with children and young people (Gibson & Cartwright, 2014; Hanley, 2009; King et al., 2006). For many of those researching and currently using digital technology as part of the therapy they offer, their findings indicate that it is possible to create an effective working alliance when working online, and much of the writing emphasises the benefits of working in this way. As Amichai-Hamburger and colleagues (2014) write:

> For many people the internet is perceived as a safer, more secure environment than the offline world, which in itself will aid in the creation of a therapeutic relationship online … the removal of face-to-face interaction may actually increase self-disclosure and honesty. Some people feel less shame and anxiety online and therefore the transition to an intimate level may be faster than in a traditional therapeutic setting. (Amichai-Hamburger et al., 2014, p. 289)

Aspects of working online, such as those mentioned above, may be of particular relevance to children and young people, who may well experience shame and anxiety regarding talking to an adult therapist "face-to-face". According to the research of Gibson and Cartwright (2014); "Young people seem particularly aware of and sensitive to power relationships and at times may experience counselling with an adult negatively as an attempt to undermine their independence" (Gibson & Cartwright, 2014, p. 97). They go on to state that; "This research, however, suggests that text counselling, from the perspective of young people, might offer greater opportunity than face-to-face counselling, for the young person to protect their autonomy" (Gibson & Cartwright, 2014, p. 103). This particular piece of research suggests that for many young people there is an increase in a sense of control over their therapy from, in this example, texting their counsellor, and that this enhances their experience of therapy. This will not of course be the case for all young people, for many of whom it is the very experience of being in the presence of an adult who is interested in them and who maintains the boundaries of the therapeutic relationship which is the most beneficial aspect of therapy.

Working with a counsellor online rather than seeing them in a traditional face-to-face setting could also have the benefit of reducing considerably parental involvement in their therapy which, as previously discussed, may be a difficulty for some young people having counselling in private practice. A young client receiving therapy online will not be dependent on their parent to transport them to sessions, or have to tolerate the anxiety that a parent is in the waiting room can overhear what they are sharing with their therapist. In this respect, online therapy in private practice could offer young people a therapeutic experience more akin to counselling in school, where parents are less involved in the practicalities of the therapy. There would most likely still need to be parental involvement in paying for sessions but this could potentially be arranged to be completed online. Contracting regarding when and how the therapy took place could be managed between client and practitioner without the need for parental involvement potentially to a greater extent than in a face-to-face setting. This could certainly have an impact on the young client's sense of autonomy regarding their therapy. Practitioners considering working in this way with young people would need to think carefully about how they contract with both parents and clients. There would need to be careful consideration of the boundaries around the timing of sessions and how to manage "no-shows" on the part of the client. Also requiring consideration would be the contracting requirements around the limits of confidentiality, as well as thinking about how the counsellor would manage a crisis or fears that the client was at risk of harm.

There is a potentially negative factor which must be taken into account when considering working via the internet with young people. It could be argued that for some young people the internet represents an escape, and potentially a way of avoiding some of the painful or more difficult aspects of existence and relationships. For the socially anxious teenager who struggles to leave their home, therapy via email may seem like an ideal solution to enabling them to receive therapy regularly. There is inherent in this strategy the danger that the symptom will be colluded with rather than worked through and therefore be resistant ultimately to treatment.

In their paper on mobile-phone counselling, referred to earlier in the chapter, Gibson and Cartwright (2014) make mention of young people finding it easier to open up when they are not confronted by a physically present therapist having live reactions to their disclosures, which they fear might make them uncomfortable. Elsewhere, those writing about email therapy have talked about the benefits of client and therapist being able to consider their responses and think them carefully through before deciding to send. There are clearly benefits to both of these ways of conducting therapy but they also miss out an element, not just of therapy, but of basic human existence, which is being in a relationship with someone who is physically present with us synchronously. This "being in the physical presence" may not always be easy or feel comfortable for clients. It may bring up all sorts of feelings in both client and therapist which, provided there is a good enough therapeutic relationship established, can be explored and understood as part of the work, and the way issues within relationships with self and other can be safely confronted and worked through.

As in all counselling and therapy work, practitioners undertaking therapeutic work with a child or young person via the internet should not do so without adequate training and supervision in place. It is important not to see only the apparent gains and benefits for working with young people over the internet without also considering what might be lost through such an engagement. Practitioners need to hold a balance, avoiding a total resistance to working online without being seduced into it, regardless of its appropriateness with a given client, or therapeutic situation.

Establishing and maintaining a responsible online presence

The third and final part of this chapter focusses on an area which carries potential for creating either great anxiety or excitement in practitioners when they come to consider it; that of how or whether to present themselves professionally and personally on the internet. The reaction experienced may arguably depend on where practitioners identify in terms of "Digital Native" and "Digital Immigrant", a point made by Balick (2014) in the following;

> Many Digital Immigrants have taken to expressing themselves
> digitally with ease; for others, online engagement is an alienating

and sometimes frightening experience because it runs contrary to received wisdom about notions of intimacy, privacy, and exposure. However, it cannot be emphasised enough that, as a rule, this is not how Digital Natives feel about it. (Balick, 2014, p. 131)

Although a psychotherapist himself, Balick is not directly addressing his words here to the profession, although they are highly relevant to therapy practitioners who have historically tried to maintain a "blank screen" presentation in the therapy room, with generally as little disclosure of the self which exists outside the therapy room as possible. Therapists may therefore feel reticent regarding presenting themselves online in any way, imagining that this could place an unbearable strain on the client who receives so little information about them in their sessions.

At the same time, therapists may also view the internet and social networking sites as offering huge potential in terms of the ability to advertise their services in the digital marketplace, and of facilitating connections with other professionals, thus allowing them to exchange skills and knowledge with a far wider network than is possible without the web. Some practitioners may feel compelled as a result of this to build an impressive "web-presence" for themselves in order to compete with other professionals locally who are advertising and presenting themselves and their ideas online.

Balick (2014) makes the point in the above quote that it is unlikely that "Digital Natives", who represent the client group under consideration in this book, have such reticence about presenting themselves online. Children and young people coming for counselling may feel confused by a therapist who has no such online existence at all, and who seems baffled or terrified by the prospect. There is nothing to say that this perceived difference should compel practitioners to reactively start engaging energetically in social networking. Indeed, there is great value in being able to explore a client's feelings regarding their own online identity by hearing their thoughts and feelings regarding their therapist's lack of one. Working with difference is an important part of any therapist's practice, and here is no exception. The important thing here is that the client feels that the "difference" can be worked with and that they don't feel they are speaking a "foreign" language to a xenophobic therapist!

For those practitioners who wish to create and maintain an online presence there are some important factors to be considered. Table 7.1

below shows a section of the BACP Guidelines for online counselling and psychotherapy regarding maintaining a responsible online presence for practitioners:

Table 7.1. BACP Guidelines for online counselling and psychotherapy.
BACP Guidelines for online counselling and psychotherapy   **3.3 Maintaining a responsible online presence**   The online world, generally known as cyberspace, has recently seen a surge in technological interfaces such as blogs, mini-blogs, wiki's, and social networking sites. Practitioners need to be aware of client access to public profiles and personal information that can be held on these types of website. Publicly accessible personal information should remain professional and be created with the reputation of the profession itself in mind. Practitioners should be aware that they do not control what is posted by others, including material relating to their personal lives, which may be accessed by their clients and colleagues.   Maintaining a responsible online presence means the practitioner having a policy in place for dealing with events which could include: • A client requesting connection via a social networking site.   • A client blogging about their therapy and/or the therapist, possibly cutting and pasting session material.   • A client commenting on the practitioner's blog.   • A client visiting (uncontracted) the practitioner's virtual reality office or home in environments such as Second Life.   • A client editing a wiki with derogatory remarks about therapy and/or the therapist.   • The disadvantages, as well as possible advantages, of the use of instant messaging and mobile phone texting by a client outside of a contract.   (BACP, 2014a)

These guidelines outline different areas for the practitioner to consider; their private and their professional lives online, where these might intersect, and how this should be managed ethically.

Practitioners are generally directed from the beginning of their training to consider carefully the impact of intersections between their private and professional lives upon therapeutic work. Therapists are required to abstain from having another relationship outside of the therapy room with anyone being seen as a client and must consider carefully, from within the context of the therapy, the meaning of any chance encounter they may have with a client on the street, or in a social situation, along with trying to avoid working with anyone therapeutically with whom they may have "boundary issues", that is, know or have contact within another context. These principles relate to the uniqueness of the therapeutic relationship and are at the core of most practitioners' ethical practice. As touched upon in a previous chapter, these boundaries can sometimes be very difficult for children and young people to understand and need to be discussed at the initial contracting stage in order to manage carefully difficult feelings or confusions created by the difference between the relationship they have with their counsellor and that which they have with other people in their lives. Just as a practitioner might have to manage therapeutically a young client's request that they attend their birthday party or dance performance along with the other significant people in their life, now they may also be required to manage the same client's request that they befriend them on Facebook, or follow them on Twitter or Tumblr. One of the main differences regarding these therapeutic boundaries to be encountered in the context of the digital world is that of the increased potential for clients to have far greater access to information regarding their therapist via online sources. This can potentially be information which falls within or without the therapist's explicit control, and includes the client's ability to share their own thoughts and feelings regarding their therapist and therapy with a wide online audience should they so choose. Although no one can completely control what appears via an online search of their name, it is important that therapy practitioners, and in particular those working with children and young people, consider carefully how they are presented online. This may seem like a lot to ask, and perhaps even an infringement of the therapist's right to have a private life online and separate identity from that of "counsellor", but the reality is that the nature of the digital world makes it harder to have such a separate life when it is able to be accessed by those with whom we interact with in a professional capacity. As stated in the BACP guidelines (2014a) shown above; "Publicly accessible personal information should remain professional and be created with the reputation of the profession itself in mind" (BACP, 2014a, 3.3).

Personal lives online—Digital citizenship

Of course, many social networking sites have controls and privacy settings which are relatively simple to access and change, so it is possible to have a Facebook page, for example, where the user can select who their posts and profile are visible to, and remain hidden from everyone else. This can be a useful way for a practitioner to maintain a private social networking profile where they can share their life with family and friends, without necessarily being seen by clients or other members of the public. Users can also change the "audience" they share with for everything they post, so it is possible to share some of what they post with anyone and some only with "friends" or even "close friends". Practitioners having an understanding of this can be very useful in helping children and young people understand that even in cyberspace they may want to control who they share certain information or images with, and that there are ways of controlling this which they may not be aware of, or understand the importance of. Palfrey and Gasser (2008) examine in some detail the reasons why young people are so willing to share information about themselves online and make the following point; "There is reason to believe that young people systematically underestimate the risks of disclosure" (Palfrey and Gasser, 2008, p. 24). This has the potential of leaving young people open to the risk of exploitation by those with access to their personal information including cyber bullying and other abuse.

It is by no means necessary for therapists to have their own Facebook or other social network service profile, but an understanding of how they operate is invaluable when working with children and young people who are likely to have multiple "profiles" and identities online, and often run into difficulties regarding information which they have shared or which has been shared about them in various online communities.

The following case example explores how this knowledge might be useful in practice.

Case example—Clare and Gemma

Gemma is a fourteen-year-old girl being seen by Clare in her private therapy practice due to her parents' concern regarding Gemma self-harming. Clare sees that Gemma is a bright and lively girl, who has a lot of friends in high school, but who struggles with how to express her feelings of sadness and anger, particularly regarding the recent loss of her grandmother to cancer and the death of the family cat, who had been her companion since birth. In their counselling sessions Clare and Gemma have spent some time thinking together about how Gemma might use other means of understanding and expressing these difficult feelings besides cutting herself.

Gemma is very active on social networking sites and often uses her sessions to talk with Clare about what has been happening online, both positive and negative. One week she comes to her session in a distressed state having received some upsetting replies to a post she put on Facebook talking about her feelings on the anniversary of her grandmother's death. Many of her girlfriends had posted supportive messages of care and concern for her, but others online had posted comments telling her to go hurt herself or telling her that no one cares how she feels.

In the session Gemma is devastated. She feels that she has tried to find an alternative way of sharing her feelings and that, although some of the support she received felt useful, the rude comments have left her feeling that sharing how she feels with others is not safe for her.

Clare is aware of that there are privacy settings on Facebook as she uses them herself to manage her own profile. She asks Gemma who is allowed to see what she posts and Gemma says that she has it set to only be shown to "friends". Clare then asks Gemma how many "friends" she has, to which Gemma replies that she has over four hundred. Clare then invites Gemma to think with her about what "friend" means in the context of cyberspace and social networks, and what this might mean when it comes to sharing something intimate, safely.

They think together about the idea of circles of people in our lives, and what we might share with each of them. Then they think about how to apply this to Facebook and other social networks.

Over the next few sessions Gemma begins to work at creating safer spaces online for her to share her feelings with other people. She becomes engaged by the "blogs" of other young people, especially those struggling with self-harm and eventually creates and shares her own "blog" talking about the experience of loss and grief. She begins to feel safe in expressing and sharing her feelings with those who can demonstrate care and compassion.

Gemma also becomes more circumspect about how she uses other types of social media. She still engages with her friends in conversations about their general social lives, but chooses carefully where she shares more intimate information.

In this example, Clare uses her own knowledge of social media to help Gemma find ways of protecting herself online, as well encouraging her to consider how she might begin to process her difficult feelings in safe relationships, both online and in her therapy. Although operating in a digital world, which their parents and teachers may not have as much experience of, may seem somewhat exciting to young people, it may also be the case that at times they may be pleased to find that they are not completely on their own there, and can find knowledgeable adult support for their social networking issues when they need them.

"Facebook for School Counselors" (2012) is a guidance leaflet produced by Facebook in alliance with ikeepsafe.org and the American School Counselors Association which, although written for school counsellors in the US, provides some useful advice for counsellors regarding how to manage an online profile, and also how to help young people think about their own profile and identity online.

While it is important that counsellors are not positioned as needing to tell children and young people how they should "be" online, or as somehow "policing" their social networking behaviour, there is scope for helping them think about the choices they are making and what these might mean for them in the context of the therapeutic work they are engaged in at the time.

As outlined in the BACP guidelines quoted in the table above (Table 7.1), cyberspace does increase the potential for boundary conflicts than there were prior to its existence. Therapists working therapeutically online via email or other written forms of communication will need to give consideration to ethical issues such as who their emails or texts belong to and how they ought to be managed by both therapist and client. Clients may well choose to "blog" (journal online) about their experience in therapy, with or without their therapist's explicit knowledge, and using their full name. Therapists need to consider how to hold boundaries and manage the impact of issues such as these sensitively within the therapeutic relationship.

Establishing and maintaining a professional online identity

Many therapists now choose to have a visible online professional identity which is accessible by the general public. This may take the form of a website, run by an individual therapist or with others, to advertise and promote services offered. Many such websites offer clients the means to contact the counsellor directly via a contact form through the website itself. Practitioners working with children and young people may want to design areas of the website which are particularly accessible or relevant to this group. Often it will be the parents who make the first contact whether online or not, but the website can be a useful way for them to introduce their children to the idea of coming to see a particular therapist, and being able to look at a photograph of their prospective therapist can establish a sense of familiarity before they arrive for their initial assessment.

Some practitioners may choose to include a "blog" as part of their website or other online professional presence. This can be a means of sharing information which may be of use to those who come across the website relating to mental health and wellbeing. It can also be a means by which practitioners to communicate their thoughts about areas they are particularly interested in, or research or training they are undertaking. As always, therapists need to be mindful of the impact that such a "blog" might have on their therapeutic work and consider carefully how they will manage any comments or other interactions clients have with their "blog" or other online spaces. Many sites hosting blogs will allow users to control who can see the "blog" and who can comment, meaning that it is possible to operate private "blogs" which are not visible by the general public.

Alongside websites, counsellors may also choose to advertise their services via various online counselling directories. Along with websites, these provide parents and clients with information regarding a practitioner's qualifications, accreditations, experience, and any particular areas of expertise or ways of working which may be of interest. This can be a good opportunity for practitioners to share information with prospective clients, or their parents, regarding the age groups they work with, their methods of working including any non-face-to-face therapy offered, as well as their theoretical basis and geographical location.

Professional networking

As well as using online tools to advertise their services, many therapists use the internet to make and maintain connections with other professionals or organisations, such as those offering training opportunities or professional development. There are various ways of doing this from joining sites such as LinkedIn, which allows people to share information about themselves as professionals with others in various professional networks. This can be a good way of keeping in touch with other practitioners working in similar fields as well as making new contacts which might be relevant.

Social networking sites can also be used to create and maintain a professional identity which may be viewed, depending on settings, by the public as a whole, or by selected audiences in the case of Facebook. Many therapists, training institutions, and professional bodies, as well as public figures, are active on Twitter. Twitter is a social networking site which allows users to post short messages or links up to 140 characters long. Anyone can read "tweets" posted on twitter, but only those who have registered as users can "tweet" themselves. Twitter users can choose to follow the "tweets" of users whom they find particularly useful or relevant and they can "re-tweet" their "tweets" if they wish as well as offering their own "tweets". It is important for practitioners to bear in mind that their twitter profile is accessible to anyone who goes online, and even the most "professional" presence may have a bearing on clients and impact on the therapy from time to time. Twitter does provide practitioners with a very effective way of feeling part of a network of professionals in the field as well as enabling them to keep up with the latest research or policies from relevant organisations and institutions. Twitter can also be an efficient way of learning about training on offer for professional development as well as short courses and workshops in relevant areas. A selection of useful organisations and individuals to be found on Twitter and Facebook are included in the Useful Resources section of this book.

Conclusion

There is much to be considered by practitioners working with children and young people with respect to the internet, a lot of which has been covered within this chapter. As will be obvious to all, this is an area which is moving fast, and its direction of development has been, and will continue to be, hard to predict. Recent developments in smartphone technology and its availability to many children and young people have rapidly changed young peoples' use of the internet, and no doubt there will be more of these kind of profound changes to come. Therapists are in many respects uniquely placed in being able to help children and young people think about and reflect upon the tensions between their online and "real" lives in order to make meaning and sense of their existence and identity at a crucial point in their development.

Summary

- The advance of digital technology and communication have had a profound effect on the lives of children and young people in the West.
- Children and young people now grow up and develop socially via the internet as well as in traditional environments such as school and family.
- Digital technologies may have a significant impact on how young people manage issues of autonomy and separation.
- There are both positive and negative implications of children and young peoples' digital connectivity.
- Some therapists choose to deliver therapy via the internet and see online therapies as particularly relevant to this age group.
- Online therapy is a specialism requiring specific training and supervision.
- Practitioners need to think carefully about their personal and professional identities online.
- Social networks offer opportunities for practitioners to keep in contact with other professionals and obtain up-to-date information relevant to their practice and the children and young people they are working with.

APPENDIX

Useful resources

Information:

Setting-up

BACP Information Sheet P16 "How to set up a therapy room" by Julia
 McGuiness (available at www.bacp.co.uk)
Data Protection—Information Commisioner's Office (ICO)—www.ico.
 org.uk
DBS basic disclosure:
Disclosure Scotland—www.disclosurescotland.co.uk/basicdisclosureonline
For "umbrella bodies" see:
www.dbs-ub-directory.homeoffice.gov.uk

General websites:

BACP—British Association for Counselling and Psychotherapy—
 www.BACP.co.uk
UKCP—UK council for Psychotherapy—www.psychotherapy.org.uk
COSCA—Counselling in Scotland—www.cosaca.org.uk
www.young minds.org.uk
www.minded.org.uk

www.youthaccess.org.uk—young people's advice, information, and counselling.

HM Government guidance:

2015—Working Together to Safeguard Children. A guide to inter-agency working to safeguard and promote the welfare of children.
2015—What to do if you're worried a child is being abused. Advice for practitioners.
2015—Information sharing. Advice for practitioners providing safeguarding services to children, young people, parents and carers.

Training

UKCP College of Child and Adolescent Psychotherapies
ACP (Association of Child Psychotherapists)—
www.childpsychotherapy.org.uk/about/how-to-train/training-requirements
BACP Accredited course directory—www.bacp.co.uk/accreditation/AccreditedCourseDirectory

Useful organisations

UKCP Children's Faculty (Faculty for the Psychological Health of Children)—www.childrensfaculty.org.uk

Children and young people's IAPT programme

www.cypiapt.org

Social networking guidance

Facebook for School Counselors:
http://www.ikeepsafe.org/wp-content/uploads/2012/04/Facebook-For-School-Counselors-Final-Revision1.pdf

On Twitter/Facebook

@MindEdUK—"free mental health learning for all adults with a duty of care for children and young people".

@NSPCC—National Society for the Prevention of Cruelty to Children.

@YoungMindsUK—"the leading UK charity committed to improving the emotional wellbeing and mental health of children and young people".

@BACP—British Association for Counselling and Psychotherapy.

@UKCP—UK Council for Psychotherapy.

@Counselling_UK—(CounsellingDirectory) "provides a huge support network of counsellors, enabling visitors to find a counsellor close to them and appropriate for their needs".

@ DHGovuk—(Department of Health)—"Official Twitter feed from the Department of Health".

@NICEComms "Official Twitter feed of the National Institute for Health and Care Excellence".

REFERENCES

Ainsworth, M. D. S., Blehar, M., Waters, E., & Wall, S. (1978). *Patterns of Attachment: A Psychological Study of the Strange Situation*. Hove: Psychology Press.

American Psychiatric Association. (2013). *Diagnostic and Statistical Manual of Mental Disorders, 5th edition*. Virginia: American Psychiatric Association.

Amichai-Hamburger, Y., Brunstein Klomek, A., Friedman, D., Zuckerman, O., & Shani-Sherman, T. (2014). The future of online therapy. *Computers in Human Behavior, 41*: 288–294.

Axline, V. (1947). *Play Therapy: The Inner Dynamics of Childhood*. Oxford: Houghton Mifflin.

BACP (British Association for Counselling and Psychotherapy). (2013). *Ethical Framework for Good Practice in Counselling and Psychotherapy*. BACP: Lutterworth.

BACP (British Association for Counselling and Psychotherapy). (2014a). *Guidelines for Online Counselling and Psychotherapy 3rd edition*. BACP: Lutterworth.

Balick, A. (2014). *The Psychodynamics of Social Networking: Connected-up Instantaneous Culture and the Self*. London: Karnac.

Bava, S., & Tapert, S. F. (2010). Adolescent brain development and the risk for alcohol and other drug problems. *Neuropsychology Review, 20*: 398–413.

Bion, W. R. (1959). Attacks on linking. *International Journal of Psycho-Analysis, 40*: 308–315.

Bond, T., & Mitchels, B. (2008). *Confidentiality and Record Keeping in Counselling and Psychotherapy*. London: Sage.

Bond, T., & Mitchels, B. (2011). *Legal Issues Across Counselling and Psychotherapy Settings*. London: Sage.

Bott Spillius, E. (1992). Clinical experiences of projective identification. In: R. Anderson (Ed.), *Clinical Lectures on Klein and Bion* (pp. 59–73). London: Routledge.

Bowlby, J. (1973). *Attachment and Loss, Volume 2: Separation*. London: The Hogarth Press and The Institute of Psychoanalysis [reprinted London: Pimlico, 1998].

British Psychological Society—Division of Clinical Psychology (2014). *Understanding Psychosis and Schizophrenia: Why People Sometimes Hear Voices, Believe Things that Others Find Strange, or Appear Out of Touch with Reality, and What Can Help*. Leicester: BPS.

Brottman, M. (2012). Whereof one cannot speak: Conducting psychoanalysis online. *Psychoanalytic Review, 99(1)*: 19–34.

Brown, S., Tapert, S. F., Granholm, E., & Delis, D. C. (2000). Neurocognitive functioning of adolescents: Effects of protracted alcohol use. *Alcoholism: Clinical and Experimental Research, 24*: 164–171.

Bruch, H. (1973). *Eating Disorders: Obesity, Anorexia Nervosa, and the Person Within*. New York: Basic Books.

Carr, A. (1999). *The Handbook of Child and Adolescent Clinical Psychology: A Contextual Approach*. New York, NY: Brunner-Routledge.

Crisp, A. (1983). Anorexia nervosa. *British Medical Journal, 287*: 855–858.

Cochrane-Brink, K. A., Lofchy, J. S., & Sakinofsky, I. (2000). Clinical rating scales in suicide risk assessment. *General Hospital Psychiatry, 22*: 445–451.

Cook, R. J., Erdman, J. N., & Dickens, B. M. (2007). Respecting adolescents' confidentiality and reproductive and sexual choices. *International Journal of Gynecology and Obstetrics, 98*: 182–187.

Coren, A. (1996). Brief therapy—base metal or pure gold? *Psychodynamic Counselling, 2* (1): 22–38.

Cozolino, L. (2006). *The Neuroscience of Human Relationships: Attachment & the Developing Social Brain*. New York, NY: Norton.

Daines, B., Gask, L., & Howe, A. (2007). *Medical and Psychiatric Issues for Counsellors*. London: Sage.

Daniels, D., & Jenkins, P. (2010). *Therapy with Children: Children's Rights, Confidentiality and the Law (2nd edition)*. Sage: London.

Dunn, R. A., & Guadagno, R. E. (2012). My avatar and me—Gender and personality predictors of avatar-self discrepancy. *Computers in Human Behavior, 28*: 97–106.

Edwards, D. (1997). Endings. *Inscape: Formerly Inscape, 2*: 49–56.

Erikson, E. (1950). *Childhood and Society (2nd revised edition)*. New York, NY: Norton. [Reprinted London: Vintage 1995].

Erikson, E. (1968). *Identity: Youth and Crisis*. London: Faber & Faber. [Reprinted London: Faber 1971].

Fairbairn, W. R. D. (1952). *Psychoanalytic Studies of the Personality*. London: Routledge.

Fonagy, P., Cottrell, D., Phillips, J., Bevington, D., Glaser, D., & Allison, E. (2014). *What Works for Whom: A Critical Review of Treatments for Children and Adolescents (2nd edition)*. London: Guildford Press.

Freud, A. (1965). *The Writings of Anna Freud: Volume VI: Normality and Pathology in Childhood: Assessments of Development*. New York, NY: International Universities Press.

Freud, S. (1909b). Two case histories ("Little Hans" and the "Rat Man"). In: J. Strachey (Ed.), *The Standard Edition of the Complete Psychological Works of Sigmund Freud, Volume X* (pp. 5–149). London: The Hogarth Press and the Institute of Psycho-analysis, 1955.

Freud, S. (1916 [1915]). Introductory lectures on psycho-analysis (Parts I and II). In: J. Strachey (Ed.), *The Standard Edition of the Complete Psychological Works of Sigmund Freud, Volume X* (pp. 3–483). London: The Hogarth Press and the Institute of Psycho-analysis, 1963.

Freud, S. (1923). The ego and the id. In: J. Strachey (Ed.), *The Standard Edition of the Complete Psychological Works of Sigmund Freud, Volume XIX* (pp. 3–309). London: The Hogarth Press and the Institute of Psycho-analysis, 1961.

Furman, W., & Shaffer, L. (2003). The role of romantic relationships in adolescent development. In P. Florsheim (Ed.), *Adolescent Romantic Relations and Sexual Behavior: Theory, Research, and Practical Implications* (pp. 3–18). Lawrence Erlbaum: New Jersey.

Geddes, H. (2006). *Attachment in the Classroom: The Links Between Children's Early Experience, Emotional Well-Being and Performance in School*. London: Worth Publishing.

Geldard, D., & Geldard, K. (2002). *Counselling Children: A Practical Introduction*. Sage: London.

Gibson, K., & Cartwright, C. (2014). Young People's experience of mobile phone text counselling: Balancing connection and control. *Children and Youth Services Review 43*: 96–104.

Glenn, J. (1992). An overview of child analytic technique. In: J. Glenn (Ed.), *Child Analysis and Therapy* (pp. 3–26). New York: Jason Aronson.

Glenn, J., Sabot, L. M., & Bernstein, I. (1992). The role of the parents in child analysis. In: J. Glenn (Ed.), *Child Analysis and Therapy* (pp. 393–426). New York, NY: Jason Aronson.

Goss, A., & Anthony, K. (2009). Developments in the use of technology in counselling and psychotherapy. *British Journal of Guidance & Counselling, 37*: 223–230.

Gray, A. (1994). *An Introduction to the Therapeutic Frame*. London: Routledge.

Griffith, R. (2008). Consent and children: the law for children under sixteen. *British Journal of School Nursing, 6*: 281–284.

Hanley, T. (2009). The working alliance in online therapy with young people: preliminary findings. *British Journal of Guidance & Counselling, 37*: 257–269.

Hawkins, P., & Shoet, R. (2012). *Supervision in the Helping Professions (Supervision in Context) (4th edition)*. Maidenhead: Open University Press.

Hawton, K., Rodham, K., & Evans, E. (2006). *By Their Own Young Hand: Deliberate Self-Harm and Suicidal Ideas in Adolescents*. London: Jessica Kingsley.

Helsper, E., & Enyon, R. (2010). Digital natives: where is the evidence? *British Educational Research Journal, 36*: 503–520.

Herron, W. G., & Welt, S. R. (1992). *Money Matters: The Fee in Psychotherapy and Psychoanalysis*. New York, NY: The Guildford Press.

HM Government. (2003). Sexual Offences Act. London: HM Government.

HM Government. (2003). The Victoria Climbie Inquiry. Lord Laming. London: HM Government.

HM Government: DofH. (2004). *Best Practice Guidance for Doctors and other Health Professionals on the Provision of Advice and Treatment to Young People Under 16 on Contraception, Sexual and Reproductive Health*. London: HM Government.

HM Government: DfES. (2006). *What to do if You're Worried a Child is Being Abused: Departmental Advice Providing Best Practice Information for Those who Work with Children in Order to Safeguard their Welfare*. London: HM Government.

HM Government: DFCS. (2010). *Every Child Matters*. London: HM Government.

HM Government: DfES. (2015). *Working Together to Safeguard Children: Statutory Guidance on Inter-agency Working to Safeguard and Promote the Welfare of Children*. London: HM Government.

HM Government: DfES. (2015). *Information Sharing: Advice for Practitioners providing safeguarding services to children, young people, parents and carers*. London: HM Government.

Hollinghurst, S., Peters, T., Kaur, S., Wiles, N., Lewis, G., & Kessler, D. (2010). Cost-effectiveness of therapist-delivered online cognitive–behavioural therapy for depression: randomised controlled trial. *The British Journal of Psychiatry, 197*: 297–304.

Isaacs, M. B., Montalvo, B., & Abelsohn, D. (1986). *The Difficult Divorce: Therapy for Children and Families*. New York, NY: Basic Books.

Israeli, E., Asulin-Simhon, Z., & Sharabany, R. (2013). The interface between cyberspace and psychotherapeutic space: relationship avoidance and intimacy in adolescent psychotherapy. *The Psychoanalytic Study of the Child, 67:* 279–297.

Jenkins, P. (2005a). Client confidentiality and data protection. In: R. Tribe & J. Morrissey (Eds.), *Handbook of Professional and Ethical Practice for Psychologists, Counsellors, and Psychotherapists* (pp. 63–75). Hove, England: Brunner-Routledge.

Jenkins, P. (2005b). The legal context of therapy. In: R. Tribe & J. Morrissey (Eds.), *Handbook of Professional and Ethical Practice for Psychologists, Counsellors, and Psychotherapists* (pp. 77–89). Hove, England: Brunner-Routledge.

Jenkins, P. (2007). *Counselling, Psychotherapy and the Law.* London: Sage.

Kalmakis, K. A. (2010). Cycle of sexual assault and women's alcohol misuse. *Journal of the American Academy of Nurse Practitioners, 22:* 661–667.

King, R., Bambling, M., Lloyd, C., Gomurra, R., Smith, S. Reid, W., & Wegner, K. (2006). Online counselling: The motives and experiences of young people who choose the internet instead of face to face or telephone counselling. *Counselling and Psychotherapy Research, 6:* 169–174.

Kloess, J., Beech, A., & Harkins, L. (2014). Online child sexual exploitation: prevalence, process, and offender characteristics. *Trauma, Violence and Abuse, 15:* 126–139.

Kotchik, B., Shaffer, A., & Forehand, R. (2001). Adolescent sexual risk behavior: a multi-system perspective. *Clinical Psychology Review, 21:* 493–519.

Langs, R. (1998). *Ground Rules in Psychotherapy and Counselling.* London: Karnac.

Laufer, M. (1997). Developmental breakdown in adolescence: problems of understanding and helping. In: M. Laufer (Ed.), *Adolescent Breakdown and Beyond* (pp. 3–15). London: Karnac.

Lee, H., & Jureidini, J. (2013). Emerging psychosis in adolescents: a practical guide. *Australian Family Physician, 42:* 624–627.

Levenkron, S. (2006). *Cutting: Understanding and Overcoming Self-Mutilation.* New York, NY: Norton.

McCartan, K. F., & McAlister, R. (2012). Mobile phone technology and sexual abuse. *Information & Communications Technology Law, 21:* 257–268.

Marks Mishne, J. (1983). *Clinical Work with Children.* New York, NY: The Free Press (Macmillan).

Marks Mishne, J. (1986). *Clinical Work with Adolescents.* New York, NY: The Free Press (Macmillan).

Mellor-Clark, J., Barkham, M., Connell, J., & Evans, C. (1999). Practice-based evidence and need for a standardised evaluation system: Informing the design of the CORE system. *European Journal of Psychotherapy, Counselling and Health, 2:* 357–374.

Mesch, G. (2012). Technology and youth. *New Directions for Youth Development, 135*: 97–105.

Messer, J. M., & Fremouw, W. J. (2008). A critical review of explanatory models for self-mutilating behaviors in adolescents. *Clinical Psychology Review 28:* 162–178.

Mirza, K. A. H., & Mirza, S. (2008). Adolescent substance misuse. *Psychiatry,* 7: 357–362.

Neubauer, P. B. (1992). The opening phase of child analysis. In: J. Glenn (Ed.), *Child Analysis and Therapy* (pp. 263–274). New York, NY: Jason Aronson.

Oaklander, V. (1978). *Windows to Our Children: A Gestalt Therapy Approach to Children and Adolescents.* California: Real Peoples Press.

Oxford University Press (2014). *OED Online.* Oxford: Oxford University Press.

Palfrey, J., & Gasser, U. (2008). *Born Digital: Understanding the First Generation of Digital Natives.* New York, NY: Basic Books.

Palmer Barnes, F. (1998). *Complaints and Grievances in Psychotherapy: A Handbook of Ethical Practice.* London: Taylor and Francis.

Pape, H. (2014). Sexual assault while too intoxicated to resist: a general population study of Norwegian teenage girls. *BMC public health, 14*: 406 (1–9).

Piaget, J. (1964). Development and learning. *Journal of Research in Science Teaching, 2*: 176–186.

Poynton, L. E. (1997). *The Romance of Risk: Why Teenagers do the Things They Do.* New York, NY: Basic Books.

Prensky, M. (2001). Digital natives, digital immigrants. *On the Horizon, 9*: 1–6.

Ringrose, J., Gill, R., Livingstone, S., & Harvey, L. (2012). *A Qualitative Study of Children, Young People and "Sexting".* London: NSPCC.

Ross, A. O. (1958). Confidentiality in child guidance treatment. In: M. Haworth (Ed.), *Child Psychotherapy: Practice and Theory* (pp. 80–90). New York, NY: Basic Books, 1964.

Sabri, B., Coohey, C., & Campbell, J. (2012). Multiple victimization experiences, resources, and co-occurring mental health problems among substance-using adolescents. *Violence and Victims, 27*: 744–763.

Salzberger-Wittenberg, I., Henry, G., & Osborne, E. (1983). *The Emotional Experience of Teaching and Learning.* London: Routledge & Kegan Paul.

Selekman, M. (2006). *Working with Self-Harming Adolescents: A Collaborative, Strengths-Based Approach.* New York, NY: Norton.

Shefler, G. (2000). Time-limited psychotherapy with adolescents. *The Journal of Psychotherapy Practice and Research, 9*: 88–99.

Simpson, B. (2013). Challenging childhood, challenging children: Children's rights and sexting. *Sexualities, 16*: 690–709.

Skegg, K. (2005). Self-harm. *The Lancet, 366*: 1471–1483.

Steinberger, C. (2009). Cyberspace: The nodal self in the wide wide world-adolescents signing-on. *Psychoanalytic Review, 96*(1): 129–144.

Steinfeld, C., Ellison, N., & Lampe, C. (2008). Social capital, self-esteem, and use of online social network sites: A longitudinal study. *Journal of Applied Developmental Psychology, 29*: 434–445.

Stortelder, F., & Ploegmakers-Burg, M. (2010). Adolescence and the reorganization of infant defences: A neuro-psychoanalytical model. *Journal of the American Academy of Psychoanalysis and Dynamic Psychiatry 38*: 503–531.

Tantam, D. (1995). Why assess. In: C. Mace (Ed.), *The Art and Science of Assessment in Psychotherapy* (pp. 8–26). London: Routledge.

Thompson, P. (2013). The digital natives as learners: Technology use patterns and approaches to learning. *Computers in Education, 65*: 12–53.

Tucker, P. (2009). Substance misuse and early psychosis. *Australasian Psychiatry, 17*: 291.

Turkle, S. (2004). Whither psychoanalysis in computer culture? *Psychoanalytic Psychology, 21*(1): 16–30.

Turkle, S. (2011). *Alone Together: Why We Expect More from Technology and Less From Each Other*. New York. NY: Basic Books.

UKCP (United Kingdom Council for Psychotherapy). (2009). *UKCP Ethical Principles and Code of Professional Conduct*. London: UKCP.

U.S. Department of Health and Human Services, Children's Bureau. Child Welfare Information Gateway. (2014). *Mandatory Reporters of Child Abuse and Neglect*. Washington DC: U.S. Department of Health and Human Services.

Valkenburg, P., & Peter, J. (2007). Internet communication and its relation to well-being: identifying some underlying mechanisms. *Media Psychology, 9*: 43–58.

Wade, D., Harrigan, S., Edwards, J., Burgess, P. M., Whelan, G., & McGorry, P. D. (2006). Substance misuse in first-episode psychosis: 15-month prospective follow-up study. *British Journal of Psychiatry, 189*: 229–234.

Wallerstein, J. S., & Kelly, J. B. (1980). *Surviving the Breakup: How Children and Parents Cope With Divorce*. New York, NY: Basic Books.

Weisleder, P. (2004). The rights of minors to confidentiality and informed consent. *Journal of Child Neurology, 19*: 145–148.

Werkele, C., & Avgoustis, E. (2003). Child maltreatment, adolescent dating and adolescent dating violence. In: P. Florsheim (Ed.), *Adolescent Romantic Relations and Sexual Behavior: Theory, Research, and Practical Implications* (pp. 213–235). New Jersey: Lawrence Erlbaum.

Wilkinson, M. (2006). *Coming Into Mind. The Mind-Brain Relationship: A Jungian Perspective*. Hove: Routledge.

Winnicott, D. W. (1963). Psychotherapy of character disorders. In: *The Maturational Processes and the Facilitating Environment* (pp. 203–216). London: The Hogarth Press (Reprinted London: Karnac, 1990).

World Health Organisation. (1992). *The ICD-10 Classification of Mental and Behavioural Disorders: Clinical Descriptions and Diagnostic Guidelines.* Geneva: World Health Organisation.

Zetzel, E. R. (1956). Current concepts of transference. *International Journal of Psychoanalysis, 37*: 369–376.

Web resources

BACP (British Association for Counselling and Psychotherapy). (2014b). Attitudes to Counselling and Psychotherapy: Key findings of our 2014 survey. Online at: www.bacp.co.uk last accessed 7 February 2015.

Center on the Developing Child at Harvard University. (2009). Maternal depression can undermine the development of young children: Working paper No. 8. Online at: www.developingchild.harvard.edu last accessed 22 June 2015.

Facebook, ikeepsafe.org and American School Counselor Association (2012). Facebook for school counselors. www.ikeepsafe.org/wp-content/uploads/2012/04/Facebook-For-School-Counselors-Final-Revision1.pdf last accessed 22 June 2015.

INDEX